Award-Winning
Small-Space Gardens

Created and designed
by the editorial staff
of ORTHO books

Written by
Michael MacCaskey

Edited by
A. Cort Sinnes

Art direction
and design by
James Stockton

Illustrations by
Mark Pechenik

Photography by
John Blaustein
Michael Landis
Michael McKinley
Fred Kaplan
Ken Garrett

Front cover photo by
Wolf von dem Bussche

Ortho Books

Manager, Ortho Books
Robert L. Iacopi

Editorial Director
Min S. Yee

Editor
Marian E. May

Production Editor
Anne Coolman

Administrative Assistant
Judith C. Pillon

Designer
Craig Bergquist

Copy Editing by
Shirley Manning

Proofreading by
Editcetera
Berkeley, CA

Indexing by
Baxter & Stimson

Typography by
Terry Robinson & Co.
San Francisco, CA

Color Separations by
Color Tech Corp.
Redwood City, CA

Printed by
Webcrafters, Inc.
Madison, WI

Cover printed by
Graphic Enterprises
of Milwaukee, Inc.
Milwaukee, WI

Address all inquiries to:
Ortho Books
Chevron Chemical Company
Consumer Products Division
575 Market Street
San Francisco, CA 94105

1 2 3 4 5 6 7 8 9 10

ISBN 0-917102-81-9.

Library of Congress Catalog
Card Number 79-52991

Acknowledgements

Jimmy Amster, New York, NY—Page 30
William Aplin, Ventura, CA—Page 81
The Beatty's, Yountville, CA—Page 39 (top left)
Melvin Belli Office, San Francisco, CA—Page 32 (top right)
Tommy Church Design, the Bond's, Honolulu, HA—Page 8 (right), Page 35 (top left)
Horace Clay, Honolulu, HA—Page 39 (bottom right)
Michael Faskett, Napa, CA—Page 38
Rudy Harbour, Atlantic Nurseries, Long Island, NY—Page 66 (top)
Louis Hicks, Tiburon, CA
Kathy Hoffman, The French Laundry, Yountville, CA—Page 47 (top left)
Honolulu Garden Club, HA—Page 9
James Hubbard Design, Honolulu, HA—Page 8 (left), Page 64 (top right)
Haruo Kaneshiro, Honolulu, HA—Page 12, Page 26
Joshua and Mary Landis, Rutherford, CA—Page 74
Henry Leuthardt Nurseries, Inc., Long Island, NY—Page 62 (right), Pages 82 and 83
David Loring, Los Altos, CA—Page 74
Roger Mackaness, Troutdale, OR—Page 29
Rosemary Menninger, San Francisco, CA
Muriel and Arthur Orans, Horticultural Photography, Corvallis, OR—Page 31
Ed Nishida, Pearl City, HA—Page 39 (bottom left)
Dr. Rocky, New York, NY—Page 62 (right), Pages 82 and 83
Robert and Toshio Saburomaro, East Palo Alto, CA—Pages 24 and 25
Mrs. Christopher Schwemmer, Pasadena, CA—Page 17 (bottom left)
Roberto Soloria, Rutherford, CA
Marion and Mike Uyeno, Honolulu, HA—Page 27 (top right and middle), Page 39 (top right)
David Whiting, St. Helena, CA—Page 80
David Woosey Design, Honolulu, HA—Page 69

Front cover photo:
Back yard garden of George Stewart
San Francisco, CA

Back cover photo:
Rooftop garden of Libby Stewart
Grand Prize Winner
Philadelphia, PA

Judges—Small-Space Gardening Contest

Richard W. Lighty,
President, AABGA
Coordinator, Longwood Program

Mildred Mathias,
Executive Director, AABGA
UCLA Botanical Garden

Francis Ching
Vice-President, AABGA
Director, Los Angeles County
Department of Arboreta & Botanic Gardens

Patrick Seymour,
Board of Directors, AABGA
Director, Devonian Botanic Garden

Fred Widmoyer,
Secretary-Treasurer, AABGA
Chairman, Department of Horticulture,
New Mexico State University

Robert Montgomery,
Editor, AABGA Bulletin
Director, John J. Tyler Arboretum

Alan Goldowski,
Director of Horticulture
Missouri Botanical Garden

Web Crowley
Morton Arboretum,
Lisle, Illinois

Award-Winning Small-Space Gardens

Small Gardens

Every family can have a garden. If there is not a foot of land, there are porches or windows. Wherever there is sunlight, plants may be made to grow.
Page 5

No Space

Where do you make a garden if you have no outdoor garden space? There is room on most balconies or indoors. What about the rooftop?
Page 54

Techniques

The basics of small space gardening: container gardening, raised beds, and training. Special sections on bonsai, mame bonsai, and trough gardening.
Page 13

Big Harvests

The highest quality fruits and vegetables can be harvested from the smallest of spaces. The possibilities are endless.
Page 75

Small Space

What to do with a limited amount of outdoor garden space. Here are some common landscape problems and solutions.
Page 31

Notebook

Our ideas and recommendations for the best trees, shrubs, ground covers, vines, perennials, and annuals for small gardens.
Page 89

Small Gardens

*"Every family can have a garden. If there is
not a foot of land, there are porches or
windows. Whenever there is sunlight, plants
may be made to grow; and one plant in a
tin-can may be a more helpful and inspiring
garden to some mind than a whole acre
of lawn and flowers may be to another."*

L. H. Bailey, *Garden-Making,* 1898

After talking with many small-space gardeners, we came to the necessary conclusion that a garden is a garden no matter what size it is. The amount of space one has may determine many physical aspects of the garden, but space alone is not the final determinant of whether or not a garden will be made: a strong desire for green growing plants can create a garden literally in thin air.

But the word *small* is a relative term. In the process of writing this book we had to decide whether or not to define exactly what a "small space" was. Each of us has our own set of standards. For one of the editors, *small* was anything smaller than a suburban lot; for another it was the classic city lot, long and narrow with almost no gardening space in front and a small plot in the back; another person equated small with the enclosed patios, front and back, typical of many new townhouse designs. While we think you'll agree that most of the gardens featured in this book are indeed small, we finally ended by hedging the question and accepting one gardener's definition: "small is any space you wish you had more of."

In researching material for the historical precedence of small gardens we soon realized that the definition of large and small spaces is cyclic, and that once again, gardens are getting smaller.

In 1929 *The Design of Small Properties* was published. It was part of the famous Rural Science Series edited by L. H. Bailey. The book consisted of many sample plans for what were then considered small spaces. In the introduction we read the following:

"It is a tendency of American families to leave the city apartments to make a home in the suburbs where there is play space for the children, freedom and privacy for them all. Realizing this desire, the plans that follow have been prepared to meet the living conditions of just such families. Typical house plans have been chosen to make the landscape plans as practical as possible. The designs in this book are simple, as they should be for small places, so that the first cost and that of maintenance may not be excessive; they are intended to be usable economical schemes for the average city and suburban homes."

Young gardeners today tend to think of urban spaces as being small, especially when compared with the relative spaciousness of suburban lots. Families that return to urban centers to be closer to work and less dependent on the automobile are discovering that many city lots force them into new types of gardening. And as open land becomes a more precious commodity, more townhouse, condominium and other multiple family dwellings will be built to maximize the use of the available space, and will, in turn, define "new" small spaces for homeowners and gardeners.

Before the advent of mass irrigation systems, almost all gardens were what contemporary gardeners would call small. Large gardens could exist in countries where rainfall was abundant, as evidenced by the estate gardens in England, but for the most part, the size of a garden was limited by the amount of water one could easily supply. As we enter an era when conservation of all resources is an increasing concern, it's only natural that the size of gardens would shrink once again. But size doesn't necessarily limit beauty, usefulness, or ingenuity, as we found out when we initiated the Small-Space Gardening Contest.

A small sitting garden in a greenhouse-like atmosphere creates a impressive effect in a minimum of space.

The contest

In an effort to find out how gardeners were actually gardening in small spaces, we decided to hold a contest aimed specially at this select group. Letters describing the contest were written, advertisements placed in gardening magazines, and garden clubs were contacted: the response was eager and encouraging. Several hundred applicants sent in written descriptions, as well as photographs, slides or drawings of their gardens.

The entries were cataloged and taken to a meeting of the Directors of the American Association of Botanical Gardens and Arboreta for judging. The directors came from various parts of the United States and Canada, but they all shared a common ground: a long, personal commitment to the growing of plants, and an extensive knowledge of gardening and garden design.

At the end of two days of judging there were 14 winners: one Grand Prize, five First Prizes, and eight Awards of Merit. Eight of these gardens are featured throughout the book on the pages where they are most appropriate. Gardens of the following participants received awards. Page numbers note where in the book the winners appear.

Libbie Lovett Stewart
Philadelphia, PA
Grand Prize, rooftop
garden
(page 58 and 59)

Stephen Tollefson
San Francisco, CA
First Prize, balcony
garden (page 61)

Marie Tietjens
Blue Bell, PA
First Prize, shade
garden (page 52)

Sid and Jean Pidgeon
Aloha, OR
First Prize, entry
garden
(page 33)

Theresa Duynstee
St. Catherines, Ontario
First Prize, north-
facing balcony

Nancy Chute and
Fred W. Sinon
Darien, CT
First Prize, watering
system

Kermit Hildahl
Hannibal, MO
Award of Merit, stair-
case greenhouse

Joseph William
Brannon
Highland Heights, OH
Award of Merit,
window greenhouse

Lyall Rudderham
Hamilton, Ontario
Award of Merit,
hydroponic system

Laura Bentley
Lawrenceville, NJ
Award of Merit, rooftop
greenhouse
(page 57)

Kathleen Buchanan
Valley Forge, PA
Award of Merit,
house garden (page 71)

Joseph F. Landsberger
St. Paul, MN
Award of Merit,
house garden
(page 71)

Jack Hoogenboom
St. Catherines, Ontario
Award of Merit,
sideyard

John Webster
Baltimore, Maryland
Award of Merit,
sideyard (page 40)

Four of the Directors of the American Association of Botanical Gardens and Arboreta: from the top, Robert Montgomery, Director of the John J. Tyler Arboretum, Pennsylvania; next, Richard W. Lighty, Coordinator, Longwood Program, Pennsylvania; right, Fred Widmoyer, Chairman, Department of Horticulture, New Mexico State University; below, Mildred Mathias, Director, Botanical Garden University of California at Los Angeles. Opposite page: Inside the rooftop greenhouse of Award of Merit winner, Laura Bentley, are *Cattleya* orchids.

If you missed participating in this contest, there will be similar competitions in the future, on various aspects of gardening. Watch for announcements in garden magazines, nurseries and garden club bulletins.

Design versus style

The words *design* and *style* are slippery words that evade easy definition. For the person planning a garden, though, it is important to make a distinction between the ideas contained in the two words.

The design of a garden, no matter what its size, is the backbone of the garden. The overall size of the garden area, the location and size of the lawn, pathways, fences, pool, deck, patio, planting areas, plants and trees, and any other physical element of the plan are all determined by the needs of the people using the garden, the unalterable elements of the space (a large tree, a steep slope, an outcropping of rocks), and the ability of the person making the design or plan.

When an architect or designer looks over a completed project, you'll often hear the somewhat mysterious phrase "it works" or "it doesn't work." It's hard to imagine a design *working*, but when a design is good—that is, when it relates to its surroundings in size and scale, makes good use of materials, and enables the owners to do what they had intended to do—a design can indeed *work*.

The style of a garden is another consideration altogether. Several different gardens can have the same basic design but entirely different styles. A pool can be free form or classically Roman. A pathway can be cobblestones, brick, tanbark, or railroad ties. The landscape plan may rely on classical symmetry or use the wild and cluttered English cottage garden as its inspiration. Style is a personal preference. A Japanese style garden is not inherently "better" than a Spanish style patio garden. The appeal of one style over another is the subject of long and heated discussions leading nowhere. We respected the admonition of one gardener we visited whose garden was a somewhat unorthodox mixture of styles: "It's my garden and you don't have to like it."

All this is not intended to mean that if you don't have a design or style to your garden you can't have a garden—obviously you can. Many gardeners are content to have a mixture of green growing, flowering, and fruiting plants, with no particular rhyme or reason. Others yearn for a garden with a particular style—something remembered from childhood, from travels, ideas "stolen" from a neighbor across town, or a fantasy never seen before.

Another type of gardener, and these are not mutually exclusive groups, needs a garden to meet specific requirements: to house a bonsai collection, provide an adequate play area for kids, display a collection of roses, leave room for a sundeck and volleyball court, or some other personal requirement that will affect the design of the garden.

A word of advice: If you are in one or both of the above categories—someone with definite needs and/or desires but who is not sure how to go about creating what you want—take a little time before you go about making your garden. Look at the photographs on these pages, and in other books and magazines, and try to distinguish exactly what it is that you admire. Make a list, or start a file with tear sheets and photographs, and before long you will probably begin to see a pattern develop. When it comes time to go to the nursery or consult a designer, you'll be able to express your intentions more clearly and end up with a garden that is a clear expression of your needs and activities.

These similar pathways illustrate that the practical aspects of a design may be similar, while the style reflects the individuality of the owner. The overall effect of the garden on the left is one of tailored precision: the one on the right has a more rustic, informal effect. In both instances, there is a harmonious relationship between the garden style and the architecture of the home. The photograph on the right shows the classic and familiar Japanese style garden. Note that all three photographs depict the same design function—namely a pathway.

The illustration above serves as an extreme demonstration of the fact that while two different gardens can share the same basic design, their styles may be widely divergent. Below, note that a design element as subtle as *proportion* can influence style. The pool's shape, below, suggests a "Romanesque" formality although the garden itself has no distinct style.

The advantages of small space

Those who must accept the limitations of small spaces should also be aware of the advantages of small gardens. People who have previously gardened ½-acre lots and are now patio gardeners tell us that their gardening enjoyment has not been diminished, just changed. From such a gardener: "I know perfectly well that no one back home would call my garden a garden at all. *There* I had several acres to think about, plus a huge house with six bedrooms. Here in my apartment I have four rooms, including the kitchen and bath, and balcony, and just these ten plants. But look at how happy my plants are! Now that I don't have to dust under all those beds and keep changing all that shelf-lining, I have the time to baby my little garden. Last year that Christmas cactus rewarded me with three solid months of bloom . . . ."

Condensed spaces bring all plants into sharper focus, making even a common geranium in a clay pot a "specimen plant." Weeds, dead flowers and leaves, and other rubbish stand out blatantly, demanding attention. The time needed for chores is shortened in small spaces, leaving more time to actually enjoy the garden. And the advantages of small gardens are even more obvious for reluctant gardeners: with less time and effort, you can still have an attractive garden, and plenty of time left over for other activities.

The desire to garden is a hard thing to explain to someone who has never experienced it. As we visited gardens, even we were surprised at the lengths some people went to just to be able to grow a few plants. We heard of gardeners carrying sack after sack of soil up several floors to rooftop gardens, bringing huge tubs of tender plants indoors nightly during a cold spell, and of people breaking up concrete patios so there would be some bare dirt to garden in. Several times we could not help but ask "Why?" One gardener we talked to said it for many: "Why? . . . I guess you could say that I garden because I have to. Something in my makeup needs a garden, needs to grow things, needs to try different plants in unusual spots just for the fun of it, needs to work outside in the dirt. People look at my little garden and say, 'Obviously, you have a green thumb.' My usual response is that a green thumb is nothing but work, a little know-how as to suitable locations for certain plants, and a happy, heart-felt appreciation for, and cooperation with, the surprises nature comes up with."

Above: Not all gardeners see small spaces as a detriment. For some, it represents a chance to achieve a type of perfection impossible on a larger scale. Below left: Small gardens and miniature plants go hand-in-hand.

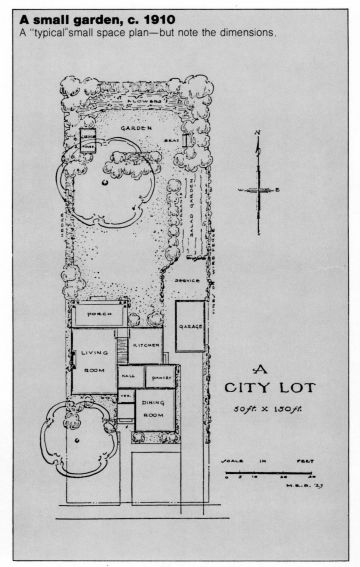

A small garden, c. 1910
A "typical" small space plan—but note the dimensions.

A CITY LOT
50 ft. x 150 ft.

SCALE IN FEET

How this book is organized

In writing this book we were faced with the space limitations of 112 pages. In deciding what to put in and what to leave out, we decided that the emphasis belonged on what was unique to small-space gardening rather than the fundamentals, which are the same in any size garden. If you need more information concerning the basics of gardening, check the suggested reading list on page 108. Specified books there will help get beginning gardeners started.

On pages 13 to 29 we've taken a close look at some of the basic elements of small-space gardening, namely, containers, and raised beds, training plants to fit small spaces, and growing miniature or dwarf plants.

The middle portion of the book is divided between gardeners who have some outdoor space to work with, and those who have only balconies, windowsills, or no space at all. *Small Space*, on pages 30 to 53, explores representative entryway gardens, side yards, mobile homes, kitchen gardens, and shade gardens. In the *No Space* chapter, pages 54 to 73, we've featured some enterprising gardens on rooftops, balconies, and decks. Also included are indoor gardening ideas, and detailed information on the old-fashioned windowbox.

Big Harvests, pages 74 to 87, shows what determined gardeners, intent on harvesting food, can do in a small area. Space-saving training and planting ideas for vegetables, fruits and berries are included.

Also included in the previously mentioned chapters are nine full-sized sample plans that deal with a number of typical small-space problems. These plans can be duplicated as is, or adapted to your own particular situation.

The *"Notebook,"* pages 88 to 107, is a simple, informal discussion of the plants most useful in limited space landscapes. Far from all-inclusive, it will bring to your attention the basic, generally most successful plants that you can use to build a plant list for your own garden.

The chapter is divided into six parts—trees, shrubs, ground covers, vines, perennials and annuals. Use our comments as a taking-off point for discussions with local nurserymen.

Our photographers quickly discovered that "small-space" gardens don't necessarily fit neat categories. For instance, the garden below—it is both a rooftop and balcony. In any case, the simple plantings surrounding the table and chairs significantly enhance the beautiful view.

Techniques

Here are the basics of small space gardening: containers, raised beds, soils, and training plants. Special sections on bonsai and trough gardening. Tips and techniques to guarantee gardening success.

Container gardening is probably the single most important gardening practice for those with limited space. On decks, rooftops, patios, balconies, narrow yards or walkways, containers bring gardening to the gardener.

Entire vegetable gardens can be containerized (see page 79). An "orchard" flourishes on a tiny balcony in New York City (see page 83). In both cases, containers of various sizes and shapes play a fundamental role.

The major advantage of container gardening is *ease:* you make or buy a container, fill it with good soil and plant whatever you want—asparagus, rhubarb, lettuce, chrysanthemums or a citrus tree. By controlling the quality of the soil you increase your chances for disease-free gardening. With a light, fast-draining, air- and water-retentive mix, almost anything can thrive. There are no weeds to battle, no rows to keep straight and no fighting with soil insects or diseases. Placed on a balcony, deck or patio right outside your kitchen door, containers can hold the freshest possible fruits, vegetables and herbs. If you move, it's a simple matter to take your containers, soil and plants with you.

Containers of every variety are available from nurseries and other suppliers, or you can make your own. Ranging from clay to plastic to wood, they all have advantages which can be utilized in different gardening situations. There are plans for a variety of containers in several of the Ortho Books.

Raised beds are also a kind of container. Usually, they are simple, big boxes made of wood, brick, stone or a variety of other materials. While some are raised completely

off the ground and supported by legs, most have no bottoms and 8 to 12-inch sides. Because they make home gardening so much easier and more successful, raised beds or a closely allied method are used by most good gardeners.

Trough gardening and the art of bonsai are two specialties that use containers and are particularly adapted to small spaces. Bonsai are plants that are dwarfed in such a way that they will imitate their full-size relatives in character. This highly refined horticultural art, developed in Asia hundreds of years ago, is described in detail on pages 24 to 25. Mame bonsai is a miniature bonsai. It's pronounced *may-may*. Take a look at pages 26 and 27 if it's hard to imagine a miniature bonsai. A mame bonsai of show quality is usually 5 years old and no taller than 6 inches. Troughs—special kinds of stone containers originally used as sinks or animal feed troughs in rural England—are illustrated on pages 28 to 29.

Another important small-space gardening practice is that of training plants to behave or grow as you desire. For instance, if you think fruit trees are too big for your space, think again. An apple grafted onto a dwarf rootstock can be trained to fill a space only 2 by 3 by 4 feet. And it is not difficult to do. Espaliers—plants trained to grow flat against a wall or trellis—can be used for a wide variety of purposes. In a shady corner, plants such as luster-leaf holly (*Ilex latifolia*) will thrive. Its flexible branches make it easy to espalier. Against a hot wall, fire thorn (*Pyracantha coccinea*) can be used in the same way. Vegetables and fruits that trail can be guided along a trellis. These include cucumber, watermelon and even pumpkins. All you need, besides a trellis or wires for the vine, is a support for the heavy fruits.

In this chapter you will find some of the gardening fundamentals you can use to make a garden in a small space.

Left: An unusual and beautiful bonsai specimen—bougainvillea. In this case, the exact age is not known but the owners guess at least 50 years old. Bonsai represents "small-space" gardening in its most sophisticated and idealized form. Making bonsai is one of the most rewarding activities for dedicated gardeners.

Containers

People have always needed plants around them. Long ago containers were used when water was scarce or soil was poor, and for bringing plants not adapted to the local climate inside for the winter.

In ancient Egypt, Greece, India and China medicinal and edible plants were container-grown. The Romans used windowboxes and rooftops for gardens. During the Middle Ages, the people of Spain, Portugal and Italy used container-grown citrus, bay laurel, oleander and other trees and shrubs as landscape accents, often grouping them near the fountain or wellhead in the courtyard.

In Asia by the 15th century, the technique of bonsai was refined, the ultimate in container gardening.

Because of our urban lifestyle and the many advantages of container gardening, plants in containers have become much more common in the United States in just the past ten years. Most of us have had some contact with them—in a houseplant gift, a living Christmas tree in a tub or a nursery purchase.

The next few pages are designed to get you started with container gardening. We'll talk about the kind of containers, about soil mixes, and about watering and fertilizing.

Kinds of containers

Anything that will hold soil is a potential container, but here the subject is narrowed down to those containers most often found in nurseries and garden centers.

Clay. These pots are by far the most common type of container. They may be the standard tapered-with-rim type but are also available in a myriad of shapes and sizes, with or without ornamental designs. The color and texture complement many plants. The clay itself is porous, allowing the exchange of air and moisture to the benefit of the roots.

A container can be anything that holds soil, but even that liberal definition is occasionally expanded upon. Pictured in this photograph is a plaque meant to be displayed vertically. The soil is held in the driftwood using wire and sphagnum moss. A miniature collection of succulents provides an interesting textural display.

With care, clay pots will last upwards of 10 years. To wash away the white crust in used pots, soak them in a solution of 1 part vinegar to 5 parts water.

Plastic. Less expensive and lighter in weight, plastic pots have gained considerable favor with commercial growers. Water does not evaporate through the sides, so is conserved. But because air can't get through plastic, mixes for plastic containers should be light and have plenty of air space.

Of the different kinds of plastic available, the heavier,

Plants that thrive in containers don't do so by accident — they need plenty of attention. Frequent watering and feeding are a must.

flexible type will last longer because it resists the degrading effects of sunlight. Any plastic container exposed to strong sunlight for very long will become brittle.

Dark colored pots will absorb considerable heat in a short period, possibly damaging roots. Plastic containers should therefore be light colored or protected from direct sunlight.

Some plastic pots are attractive but a plain one can be dressed up by building a simple wood frame to enclose it.

Wood. Here the variety possible is nearly endless, especially if you design and make your own containers. Plans for some simple wood containers can be found in several of the Ortho Books. Redwood, cypress and cedar are the woods most commonly used because they resist decay. Other long-lasting woods such as black locust or Osage orange may be locally available.

Even if a container is made of a decay-resistant wood, it will last much longer if it is treated before the soil goes in. Products containing copper naphthanate or copper sulfate will color the wood slightly green but are very effective decay preventers. If you don't want the green tone to show, use such products only on the bottom and inside. Otherwise, use a clear-drying water seal to maintain the original appearance of the wood. Or you can use a plastic liner on the inside walls of the container.

For trees and shrubs that need a large container, a wood box put together with bolts so that it can be taken apart is very handy. This kind of knock-down box makes the periodical refreshing of the soil around a heavy tree relatively simple.

Wood fiber. Made from mill waste products, these containers are attractive, practical and probably the least expensive type available. The trick is getting them to last for more than a season or two. The larger sizes (18 inches in diameter and up) are usually coated with wax to retard decay. Standard wood preservatives such as copper sulfate, copper naphthanate or water seals will considerably increase the useful life of wood fiber containers. With good care they can last as long as three to four seasons. These containers are available in a wide variety of sizes and shapes.

Ceramic. Often the most expensive, these are also the longest lasting and often the most attractive. Because of the cost, you should have both a plant and place in mind as you shop for one of these containers. If you find the perfect container but it wasn't made with drainage holes, there are two ways you can still use it. First, you can drill drainage holes. Use a carbide-tipped drill, take your time and don't force it. The alternative is to use a smaller clay pot for the plant and put it inside the ceramic one. Called double-potting, this simple arrangement makes a dripless pot that won't leave any water marks on furniture.

Wire baskets and boxes. You are probably familiar with hanging baskets made of wire and packed with unmilled sphagnum peat moss. They're handsome, but make no mistake—daily watering is necessary, especially in summer. Frequent watering also means frequent fertilizing. To save on maintenance, experiment with materials other than sphagnum moss for lining the basket. We've used plastic, indoor/outdoor carpet, felt carpet padding and combinations of these. They'll retain water longer than the moss, so save you time.

An attractive and useful container can be made with a wood frame, ½-inch mesh hardware cloth and polyethylene. Make the frame of 2 by 2s the dimensions desired. Line the inside and bottom with the hardware cloth, then use a continuous strip of polyethylene around the inside. It's simple to make, attractive and inexpensive.

Left: Some of the most satisfying of all container specimens are members of the citrus family. Top: A layer of sphagnum moss in between the clay pot and the decorative container reduces water loss. Right: Miniature hanging wire basket can be packed with sphagnum moss or other material. See text above.

Container soils

"Do I need a special soil? There's good soil in my garden—can I use it to fill containers?"

These are questions readers frequently ask and for good reason: it does seem to make sense that a good soil is a good soil whether in a container or the landscape. But containers do need a special soil.

One reason is that using garden soil may introduce disease. Success is much more likely if you begin with a totally sterile mix.

The main reason that plants in containers need a special soil is that they need fast water infiltration and good drainage. In soil, water is pulled by gravity, capillary action and the attraction of small clay particles. This water movement is dependent upon a continuous water column, like a hose syphon. Soil confined in a container has to have a loose, open structure for good drainage because the water column, or syphon, is so limited.

Plants in garden soil will grow when the rate of water infiltration is as little as ½ inch an hour. To survive in a container, the same plant needs a water infiltration rate of 5 to 10 inches an hour.

The frequently repeated advice for improving drainage—add a layer of pea gravel or other porous material to the bottom of the container—sounds logical but actually results in less air and more water at the bottom. Fill the entire container with the same mix, covering the drainage holes with a bit of screen to hold in the mix.

Along with fast drainage, a good container soil must have plenty of space for air. A garden soil in a container holds too much water and too little air, whereas the most important characteristic of a good container mix is plenty of air in the soil after drainage. A typical loam (garden soil) has less than 5 percent air space after drainage compared with over 20 percent in a mixture of peat moss and perlite.

Plants do differ in how much air they require in the soil. Some need plenty, others get along with much less.

Azaleas and ferns are typical examples of plants that need at least 20 percent air space. Vegetables such as lettuce and carrots will grow most succulent in soil with plenty of air.

Conifers, ivy grasses and roses will grow satisfactorily in soils with as little as 5 percent air space. If you must use a heavy container soil, they will tolerate it.

After you have met the requirements of fast water drainage and plenty of air space, look for a container soil that will hold onto as much water as possible. This is tricky because water retention works against fast drainage and air space. The soil that holds onto the most water will drain slowest and have little room for air. Therefore, this last requirement—water retention—is a compromise. This is easy to see in the chart above. "Total porosity" tells how fast the soil drains. The higher the number, the faster the drainage. The numbers for water retention and air space are percent by volume.

Container soil characteristics

Material	Total Porosity	Water Retention	Air Space After Drainage
Clay loam	59.6	54.9	4.7
Sphagnum peat moss	84.2	58.8	25.4
Fine sand	44.6	38.7	5.9
Redwood sawdust	77.2	49.3	27.9
Perlite, 1/16–3/16"	77.1	47.3	29.8
Vermiculite, 0–3/16"	80.5	53.0	27.5
Fir bark, 0–1/8"	69.5	38.0	31.5
1:1, fine sand: fir bark	54.6	37.4	15.2
1:1, fine sand: peat moss	56.7	47.3	9.4
1:1, perlite: peat moss	74.9	51.3	23.6

Container gardening tips

Plants growing in containers demand closer attention than the same plants growing in a flower border or a vegetable patch. When you constrict the root zone in a container, you must compensate for the smaller root area by watering and feeding more frequently. Given this fact, there are some simple tips that can help make the difference between a healthy and sick plant and between an aggravated and satisfied gardener.

Use a good soil mix. A good landscape soil does not necessarily make a good container soil. Container growing is different from ordinary garden growing, and soil for containers must have these characteristics: fast drainage of water; plenty of air in the soil after drainage; and a reservoir of water in the soil after drainage.

Avoid non-wettable soils. A common example of a non-wettable soil is milled peat moss that is completely dry. Water will still be sitting on top, not soaked in, days later. If you've had this problem, ask your nursery about wetting agents. They literally make the water wetter by reducing its surface tension. With a wetting agent in the water, the same dry peat moss is thoroughly wet within moments.

Don't overfill the container. An 8-inch pot should have about 2 inches of space at the top to hold water. Doing a good job of watering is much more difficult if you fill the pot so full with soil that an adequate amount of water cannot sit before soaking through and thoroughly wetting the container soil.

Use a mulch. A mulch (a protective covering spread over the top of the soil) is as beneficial to a container plant as to a landscape plant. It slows the drying of the soil surface and, because it prevents a crust from forming, air gets into the soil. A mulch also moderates surface temperature. Good mulches for container plants are: unmilled sphagnum peat moss, fir bark, small stones, and living plants such as Corsican mint, Scotch or Irish moss and chamomile.

Double-potting. Putting a pot with drainage holes inside a container with no drainage holes has several advantages: it avoids water leaks, it moderates the environment for the roots, and it allows you to use a very decorative outer container. A glazed ceramic outer container with no drainage holes cannot leak or sweat moisture, so is safe on furniture and carpets. (Double-potting is the technique most often used for large indoor plants in commercial office buildings.) Beyond these practical advantages, the roots of a double-potted plant are insulated from temperature extremes and evaporation is reduced.

Put a layer of gravel in the base of the exterior pot and pack the space between the two pots with perlite, unmilled sphagnum peat moss or fir bark.

Use knock-down containers for trees. Any large container is more practical if it can be taken apart. The reason: container trees must be removed from their pots every 2 or 3 years for root pruning. Otherwise, all the feeder roots bunch at the walls of the container and the plant languishes. One side of the container can be attached with screws; better yet, all sides can be screwed together for easy separation.

The basic ingredients. Special soil mixes are commonly called "synthetic" but it's the mix that is synthetic, not the ingredients. The materials are entirely natural, but they are put together in a variety of ways not normally found in nature.

Synthetic soils are composed of two parts: an organic fraction and a mineral fraction. The organic fraction may be peat moss, redwood sawdust, wood shavings, bark of hardwoods, fir or pine bark, or combinations of these.

The mineral fraction may be vermiculite, perlite, pumice, sand or a combination. Vermiculite is mined. It is originally a flaky, mica material but when exposed to high heat, it expands like an accordian. Perlite, or sponge rock, is similar. It is a granite, volcanic material that explodes like popcorn when heat treated.

Perlite, vermiculite and sand are the most common mineral materials used in synthetic soils. Peat moss was by far the most common organic material but has become so expensive in recent years that bark or other organic matter is now often used instead.

The best known synthetic soil mixes were developed by the University of California (the "U.C. mix") and Cornell University ("Cornell peat-lite mix").

Once the container-gardening bug bites, watch out—you'll be tempted to try your hand at everything from genetic dwarf peaches (top) to perennials (left) to annuals (above). Displays of colorful flowers are easy to arrange and rearrange by the season. Background greenery can be containerized and used in a more permanent fashion, as with the ferns, pictured at left.

Making a container soil

If you need only a few cubic feet of container soil, it will be less expensive to buy one of the commercial mixes than to buy the primary materials and mix them yourself. A bag containing 2 cubic feet is enough soil for 20 to 22 one-gallon containers or 35 to 40 six-inch pots. A planter 24 by 36 by 8 inches deep needs 4 cubic feet of mix. Commercial mixes are available under a wide variety of trade names — Redi-Earth, Jiffy Mix, Super Soil, Metro Mix, Pro Mix, and others.

You can modify the commercial mixes. If the mix is so light that the container tips over in a wind or the plant is not adequately supported, add sand. If the texture is so fine that the mix is not porous enough to hold air, add perlite.

One basic mix. Gardeners who believe that every type of plant requires a special soil mix find it difficult to accept the fact that a simple combination of peat moss and sand (or perlite or vermiculite) can be used for virtually all types of plants, from cacti to tropicals.

Choose the ingredients that will give the best blend for your planting program. Where the containers will receive frequent spring and fall rains, use perlite rather than vermiculite. If your mix is to be used in shrub and tree containers, add one-third sand or garden soil for a heavier mix.

Whatever the ingredients, the mixing process is the same. To make a cubic yard of soil, take:

14 cubic feet of peat moss or nitrogen-
   stabilized fir bark or pine bark and
14 cubic feet of vermiculite or perlite.

Dump the ingredients in a pile and roughly mix them with a shovel. If the peat moss has packed into clumps, use your hands to break them up. Lightly moisten the mix as you work it so that it is just damp when you are finished. Peat moss and some other organic materials are sometimes difficult to wet—the water just beads up and runs off. Warm water will more readily wet peat moss but may be not be handy to the place you are doing the mixing. A dry or liquid wetting agent will eliminate the problem.

After the major ingredients are roughly mixed into one pile, add the fertilizer:

5 pounds of dolomite or ground limestone and
5 pounds of a 5-10-10 fertilizer (5% nitrogen;
   10% phosphorus; 10% potassium; 75% filler)

The 5-10-10 fertilizer should also contain sulfur, iron, manganese and zinc. These are important nutrients that will be listed on the fertilizer label. Dolomite limestone should be favored over ordinary ground limestone because it contains magnesium, another essential plant nutrient.

Mix by shoveling all the ingredients into a cone-shaped pile, letting each shovelful dribble down the cone. To get a thoroughly mixed product, the cone building should be repeated 3 to 5 times.

Assemble the basic ingredients before preparing mix.

Measure ingredients into separate piles.

More formulas. The above mix is a basic formula. There are several variations of it for special purposes.

To make a cubic yard of a very lightweight mix for seedlings, small containers and indoor plants, mix:

9 cubic feet of vermiculite
9 cubic feet of peat moss
9 cubic feet of perlite
5 pounds of 5-10-10
5 pounds of ground limestone.

A heavier mix for seedlings and larger pots is:

7 cubic feet of fine sand
14 cubic feet of peat moss
7 cubic feet of perlite
5 pounds of 5-10-10
8 pounds of ground limestone.

A special mix for indoor plants that is widely recommended goes like this:

14 cubic feet of peat moss
7 cubic feet of vermiculite
7 cubic feet of perlite
5 pounds of 5-10-10
8 pounds of ground limestone
1 pound of iron sulfate.

Begin blending process by combining all ingredients into one pile.

Rebuild pile three to five times for thorough distribution.

Trees and shrubs that will be left outdoors need a heavier soil mix. The plants are larger and need the support of a heavy mix. Because the containers are usually larger, requiring more mix, using less expensive ingredients is wise. Two appropriate mixes are:

18 cubic feet of nitrogen-stabilized sawdust or ground bark
9 cubic feet of fine sand
5 pounds of 5-10-10
7 pounds of ground limestone
1 pound of iron sulfate.

Or

9 cubic feet of nitrogen-stabilized ground bark
9 cubic feet of fine sand
9 cubic feet of peat moss
5 pounds of 5-10-10
7 pounds of ground limestone
1 pound of iron sulfate.

In all of these formulas we have substituted a 5-10-10 fertilizer for combinations of superphosphate, calcium or potassium nitrate and other primary fertilizers. If you prefer to make your soil mix right from scratch, refer to either the Cornell Information Bulletin 43 or U.C. Manual 23 (see page 107 for ordering).

Final mix is ready for use or can be stored if mix is dry.

If you need less than one cubic yard. A cubic yard is 27 cubic feet or 22 bushels, and that's a lot of soil. In our experience, one-third of a cubic yard (9 cubic feet) is the amount that we often want to use, and therefore make, at one time.

Synthetic soil ingredients are often available in 4 or 5 cubic foot containers from nurseries and garden centers. The last mix we made for our garden started with one 5 cubic foot bag of peat moss and one 4 cubic foot bag of perlite. For this quantity, add 1 pound 10 ounces of a 5-10-10 fertilizer instead of 5 pounds, and an equal amount of dolomite or ground limestone.

When and how to fertilize a synthetic soil mix

When using a mix containing a 5-10-10 fertilizer, feeding normally should begin 3 weeks after planting. If the plant needs frequent watering, start the feeding program a little earlier.

Because fertilizers are leached through the mixes when watered, the frequency of watering helps determine the frequency of fertilizing. Fertilizers will leach faster from mixtures containing perlite than from those containing vermiculite. Therefore, plants grown in a peat moss/perlite mix will require somewhat more frequent applications of fertilizer.

The other factor that determines how frequently fertilizer is needed is how fast the plant is growing, which in turn depends on the type of plant and the season. All plants, in containers or not, need fertilizer most when growth is fastest.

Some container gardeners prefer to fertilize with a weak nutrient solution, applying it with every other irrigation. When watering plants with a nutrient solution in this manner, a safe concentration would be one-fifth the amount recommended on the label for a monthly application. If the label calls for 1 tablespoon to a gallon of water, make the dilution 1 tablespoon to 5 gallons of water.

A plant needs very little fertilizer at any one time but its need is continuous. Frequent applications of a weak nutrient solution, as described above, satisfy the constant need for nutrients. The use of time-release fertilizers is another popular method. They provide nutrients in small amounts every time the plant is watered. The labels on such products show the recommended rates of feeding.

Raised beds

One of the oldest—and newest—garden ideas is the raised bed. Throughout gardening history in England, Babylon, Rome and France—anywhere soil and water problems have made good gardens difficult—gardeners have worked out solutions using the principle of planting above the ground level. The variations are many but the results are almost invariably good.

In the perennial border and mixed flower border, developed to perfection in England, the raised-soil principle was applied in one way by giving certain sections a slight tilt in order to provide drainage for plants that were susceptible to stem rot.

Adaptations of the walled raised bed of old Spain spread to California and the Southwest. The "frame" garden, a raised bed framed by cut firs, is one of the oldest garden designs in America. It helped many a pioneer vegetable gardener in many climates. It improves drainage in heavy soils and provides depth where the natural soil is shallow. In arid and hot summer areas, water can be concentrated where it's needed.

In commercial truck farming, the furrow method—another type of raised bed planting—is common wherever vegetables are grown on poorly drained land. The furrow method allows excess water to drain, and causes the soil in the root area to warm up more quickly in the spring.

Low maintenance is one of the advantages of raised beds that makes them so well suited to modern, small gardens. Weeds are less of a problem and those that do appear are easily pulled from the loose soil without having to stoop to the ground. Pathways between beds can be carpeted with sawdust, wood bark or wood chips, or a ground cover such as chamomile.

With raised beds, your garden becomes much more an outdoor living room. Because they are more defined and orderly, raised beds help utilize every inch of a small space, allowing more space for activities. When a raised bed is made with a wide cap, it doubles as a bench.

Outdoor furniture and wheeled toys can bump against a raised bed without injuring the plants.

Located near the kitchen door, a raised bed makes an ideal spot for a small herb or salad garden (see pages 46 to 49).

A customized approach to gardening is possible with raised beds. If you are a fresh lettuce connoisseur, small beds filled with a sandy mix will provide optimum conditions for intensive production. For well-formed root crops, the mix should be loose and deep. In the garden pictured at right, a special deep, narrow box was constructed for carrots.

Vegetable gardeners have discovered that a basic advantage of raised beds is having a choice of what kind of soil to fill the bed with.

The secret of vegetable gardening is to allow the plants to grow at their maximum rate. The plants should not have to slow down for lack of water or nutrients. The best way for a home gardener to meet these requirements is with a raised bed filled with a loose, fast-draining soil mix (see page 18).

Raised beds also lengthen the vegetable-growing season because the soil in them warms earlier in the spring. Where heavy spring or fall rains are common, the fast-draining beds permit plant growth when plants at ground level would be too waterlogged to grow.

Further, raised beds filled with a rich soil mix can support more plants than would normal soil at ground level. This is because the roots can reach much deeper in the looser soil texture. Such intensive planting yields high production while it saves considerable space (See page 75 for more on food gardens.)

Specialist gardeners often find that there's no place left for the new roses or iris or dahlias, or whatever is of interest for the season. They need the kind of planting space that allows them to change their selection (and their minds). A series of raised beds is one way to get order with flexibility.

If the specialty of the gardener is shade-loving plants, the raised bed idea can be put to work in many ways. Raised beds along a fence with a lath overhead is one way. On a shaded patio or terrace, the raised bed keeps good order and cleanliness.

The specialist is likely to work long and hard around a personal plant collection. Raised beds make it easier on both backs and knees.

Walls. Centuries ago, the low dry wall was often used as a boundary of a raised bed. Curving lines and a very natural look, difficult to obtain with the wood-faced beds, are easily achieved with stone.

Many different kinds of rock will perform the job of holding a raised bed of soil. The telephone directory lists suppliers under the heading "Rock." For a lasting raised bed, you may want to make a concrete foundation and use mortar between the rocks.

The photograph shows still another alternative type of wall. The gardener cast small concrete pillars using a milk carton as a form. While the concrete was still wet, a short steel rod was pushed into it to be used as an anchor.

Many other materials can be used to make the walls of a raised bed: brick, hardware cloth, grape stakes, railroad ties, and more.

In our test gardens, we have used a waist-level-height raised bed for several years now and found it useful. Construction details are illustrated in the Ortho Book, *Wood Projects for the Garden.*

One of the more unique raised beds that we found is pictured above. A milk carton was used as a form for casting individual concrete pillars used for retaining wall. Such an arrangement testifies to the wide variety of raised bed systems that are possible.

Left, a standard raised bed. This one is bottomless and made of 2 by 10 inch stock. Additional support posts are spaced every 6 feet. Below, note solid corner bracing with ends bolted to 4 by 4 inch post.

Training

Formal pruning and training methods, common to older European gardens, are perfectly adapted to modern small gardens. With only a few demanding plants, the maintenance needed may represent exactly the right amount for the habitual gardener.

Topiary. This is the art of sculpturing plants into various shapes and figures. It was popular on large estates in England when teams of gardeners were available to maintain them. The Romans of antiquity were familiar with topiary technique. You don't need to develop topiaries on this great scale. In a small garden, one or two artistically shaped plants make a very strong accent and can be a lot of fun to develop.

Topiaries can be made either by shaping a small-leafed evergreen (such as boxwood, *Buxus microphylla japonica*, or English yew, *Taxus baccata*), or by training vining plants (such as English ivy, *Hedera helix*) along a wire frame. The latter method is faster and is the way most of the big animal topiaries are made. There's more about topiaries in Ortho's *All About Pruning*.

Some firms supply wire frames as well as established, growing topiaries. One such service is: Archetique Enterprises, 72 Eagle Rock Avenue, East Hanover, NY 07936.

A less formal type of espalier, called "tracery," is shown above. Both English and Boston ivy are well adapted to this use.

Plants to drape or climb. Another good descriptive name for these plants is "curtain plants." They function in the garden somewhat as curtains and drapes do in the home.

Plant them behind a retaining wall so the green can soften it or add texture to an otherwise barren surface. For high walls, some very effective curtain plants are: weeping forsythia (*Forsythia suspensa*), the 'Max Graf' rose, Virginia creeper (*Parthenocissus quinquefolia*) and Japanese honeysuckle (*Lonicera japonica*).

Slower-growing plants are more suitable for low walls. Groundcover junipers such as *Juniperus horizontalis* or *J. conferta* are very handsome spilling over a low wall. Creeping rosemary, *Rosmarinus officinalis* 'Prostratus,' will cling to a wall like water spilling in slow motion, and is a useful spice as well. Against a red brick wall, *Cotoneaster microphyllus* is dramatic. Its leaves are silvery, and red berries the color of the brick hang throughout winter. Similar to *Cotoneaster* is kinnikinick, *Arctostaphylos uva-ursi*. If you are interested in these kinds of plants, take a look at Ortho's *All About Ground Covers*. Characteristics that make a plant a good ground cover often make it a good draper.

English ivy is one of the most basic curtain plants. Build a 4 foot by 6 inch planter with a 4 foot trellis attached to the back and put the whole planter on wheels. Within one or two seasons, the ivy can cover the trellis and make it a handsome, movable space divider or windbreak.

Vines such as winter creeper, *Euonymus fortunei*, and Boston ivy, *Parthenocissus tricuspidata*, will grow up walls, tree trunks, along fences and the ground with very little support or encouragement. With a trellis, vines such as clematis and akebia can be trained to cover a wall from the bottom up or to drape down from the top.

Excellent fast-growing annual vines are the common morning glory, *Ipomoea purpurea*, and cup-and-saucer vine, *Cobaea scandens*. Both are easily started from seed and will cover a large trellis by midsummer.

More vines, hanging and draping, are described on pages 101 to 103.

Espaliers and wall plants. Originally the word "espalier" was defined as a trellis upon which a plant is trained. Now the expression "to espalier" means to train plants to grow flat against a wall, trellis, fence or free-standing panel. The plant may be trained into a formal pattern such as repeated horizontals, or it may be allowed to grow almost naturally to bring out the beauty of its own structure.

Choose plants that are easy to lead and start with young plants. Moderately slow growers are best. The trick is a simple one: pinch the tips of the shoots you want to slow down. You can direct growth with your fingernails and the lightest of pruning. But almost daily attention is necessary to train some plants when they are in their flush of growth.

Apples and pears are two of the most frequently espaliered plants. That's because they are amenable to this kind of training and provide the bonus of a food crop. Apricots and, in warm climates, citrus and pineapple guava are other fruits that can be espaliered.

Ornamentals to train in this fashion include the loquat, *Eriobotrya deflexa*. It has dramatic, large, bronze colored leaves and is fast growing.

Both the Southern magnolia, *Magnolia grandiflora*, and the saucer magnolia, *M. soulangiana*, are easy to train flat against a wall.

Many of the hollies respond favorably to espalier training. Notable among them is the luster-leaf holly, *Ilex latifolia*. It has large, unholly-like leaves and tolerates considerable shade. Luster-leaf holly is not hardy enough for many northern gardens but is popular in the South and is becoming more available in the West.

Fire thorn, *Pyracantha coccinea*, is one of the most commonly used wall shrubs, and for good reason. Walls that face south or west can get hot in summer and the fire thorn can take that heat. But it is widely adapted, so can also be used in the coldest as well as hottest gardens. Many varieties are available.

Espaliers are a good solution to the narrow sideyard, as described on pages 38 to 41.

Top: The old-fashioned trellis serves good purpose when space is a problem. In shady locations, the many varieties of clematis are good trellis subjects. Above: Plants with different textures and leaf colors can be used to create a repeating pattern.

23

Surgical-like tools of a bonsai master. Each has a specific use: concave pruners, wire cutters, bamboo sticks and palm bristle brush are those most used.

Bark is being peeled from this lower branch to make a "dead branch." After partially cutting, bark is torn. Result is natural look of damaged tree.

Making a dead branch that looks natural requires considerable skill. The purpose is imitation of a natural tree's struggle against adverse conditions.

Twiggy dense growth has been pruned away making the trunk more visible. Anodized aluminum wire is anchored in the root ball.

Test flexibility of branch to determine the best wire size to use. Wired branches can be bent to new shape.

Using wire properly is learned by experience. It is used to add that subtle "character" that belongs to all good bonsai.

The right pot for this tree was finally selected. Many were experimented with. Here, Tosh cuts out drain-hole covers from 1/16 inch mesh window screen.

Drain screens are anchored with eyeglass-shaped wires that Tosh quickly fashioned from training wire.

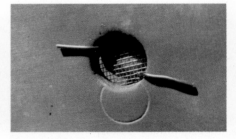
Bottom of container showing anchored screens. Without anchors, screens will shift during positioning of plant.

Specimen is removed from metal can. If possible, training is begun several months or a year before transplanting.

Soil is carefully removed using bamboo sticks. Heavy roots are removed, the small, fibrous roots are preserved if possible.

Bonsai soils are a matter of both preference and experience. This soil is 3 parts decomposed granite, 1 part each pumice rock, coarse peat and redwood compost.

Rocks to sandwich the new bonsai are carefully positioned and soil pressed underneath to hold them securely.

Bonsai

Bonsai refers to a potted plant dwarfed by special methods of culture—or to the art of growing such a plant. The word bonsai originally derived from two Chinese symbols—"bon" meaning tray or pot, and "sai" meaning to plant; hence, "bonsai," the word for container planting. But the word really means more than that. It is a highly evolved horticultural art form for which the basic techniques have been taught for over 700 years. To keep bonsai requires plenty of plant-growing know-how, and to make them you need a sensitive awareness of nature plus experience. How to gain experience? By starting.

Toshio Saburomaru has thirty years' experience at bonsai and has traveled throughout this and other countries teaching the art. He agreed to demonstrate his methods of making a bonsai. We bring his class to you.

A successful bonsai reflects or suggests the elements and forces of nature. Many bonsai show the struggle of the plant against nature: the way it barely survives clinging to rocks, adapts to the shaping forces of wind or lives even after lightning strikes.

The rocks to which a bonsai clings are mountains; the sand is either water or desert; moss implies moist, verdant qualities. All of these characteristics are apparent in the bonsai pictured on these pages.

Bonsai are an excellent outlet for the plant lover with limited space. They require relatively frequent and detailed care, satisfying the gardening urge. Very little space is needed.

To make bonsai you need to have a feel for what looks right. It is an art so largely intuitive that only certain aspects can be reduced to rules. Look at pictures in books and magazines. (Other sources of information are listed on page 109.) Most helpful of all is joining a club. There you can be instructed by more experienced bonsai growers and learn faster. Bonsai clubs exist in almost every city of this country.

Plants to bonsai

Acer buergeranum	Trident maple
Acer palmatum	Japanese maple
Cedrus atlantica 'Glauca'	Atlas cedar
Chamaecyparis obtusa	Hinoki cypress
Elaeagnus commutata	Silverberry
Juniperus californica	California juniper
Juniperus chinensis sargentii	Sargent juniper
Juniperus squamata 'Prostrata'	Prostrate juniper
Pinus parviflora	Japanese white pine
Punica granatum	Pomegranate
Quercus chrysolepis	Canyon oak
Rhododendron formosum	Formosa azalea
Taxodium mucronatum	Montezuma cypress
Ulmus parvifolia	Chinese elm
Wisteria species	Wisteria
Zelkova serrata	Japanese zelkova, saw-leaf zelkova

Moss is pressed into corners to represent cool, moist areas and give bonsai a finished look.

Right, Tosh considers the shape and character of the plant before pruning. At this point, he has already determined that the plant has a "wind-swept" shape naturally and that he should prune and train to accentuate that characteristic. Above, this initial stage of pruning and training is nearly complete. Tosh imagined a prevailing wind from the left-hand side of the picture.

Mame *(may-may)* bonsai

There are miniature bonsai that might be difficult to imagine if it were not for the pictures on this page. The word mame is a Japanese word that means "little bean." It is used to describe bonsai less than 6 inches tall.

The techniques are similar to the culture of "full size" bonsai. Doris Froning writes in the *International Bonsai Magazine*: "Even the smallest bonsai must have some training to qualify as a mame, whether by wire or just with scissors. Grown in pots sometimes as small as a thimble, the soil needs to be finer than regular bonsai soil but still needs to be well drained. Most U.S. growers use a one-third, one-third, one-third mixture containing soil, coarse grade nursery sand or fine aquarium gravel and Terragreen or Turface. The fines are sifted out."

Water. Culturally, mame bonsai are primarily distinguished by their need for frequent watering. Of course, frequency will vary with climate and exposure but in some cases, watering several times a day is necessary. An automatic mist system with a timer would be useful.

Water quality is also important. Where rainfall is plentiful, the water will contain fewer soluble salts. West of the Rocky Mountains, water is often high in salts. In those areas, rain water collected during the rainy season and stored would be very beneficial. Otherwise it may be necessary to purchase purified bottled water.

Soil. Because of the quantity of water applied, soil in the mame bonsai garden must be fast draining. As is true in many aspects of bonsai, every grower has a favorite formula. You will need to experiment to discover what works best for you. Usually sieves are used to separate soil particles of different sizes. For mame bonsai, three screens are used. The smallest is ⅛-inch mesh, then there is ¼-inch, and the largest is ½-inch mesh. Soil that does not pass through the largest screen is discarded, as is soil that does pass through the smallest. Use soil that is sterile and very infertile (subsoil) so that you can control the feeding of the plants.

How long will they live? Because the requirements of mame bonsai are exacting, you may have to do some experimenting at first. Gradually, you will find some plants that are easier to grow than others, a soil mix that works for you, and a watering regime that is practical. Once the needs of mame bonsai are understood and met, nothing prevents their living for many years. A typical mame bonsai reaches "show quality" after 5 years and there are many in existence several times older than that.

Plants for mame bonsai

Acer buergeranum	Trident maple
Adenanthera pavonina	Coralwood, sandlewood tree
Cryptomeria japonica	Japanese cedar
Ilex crenata	Japanese holly
Juniperus chinensis sargentii	Sargent juniper
Pinus densiflora	Japanese red pine
Pinus parviflora	Japanese white pine
Pinus thunbergiana	Japanese black pine
Rhododendron indicum	Macranthum azalea
Zelkova serrata	Japanese zelkova, saw-leaf zelkova

By placing this mame bonsai collection in a tray, watering becomes a much simpler chore. This grouping shows the wide variety of plants that are commonly used to make mame bonsai.

One of the smallest mame bonsai we found was this boxwood *(Buxus sempervirens)* in the "thimble" pot at left. Check with mail order suppliers for miniscule pots. Above, note the handsome displays. Below, the pruning shears point to a somewhat older boxwood.

Trough gardens

Troughs are a special kind of container. They originated as kitchen sinks or feed or water troughs for farm animals. Made of native limestone or sandstone, they were common throughout rural England for many centuries. Then, someone had the idea of adding drainage holes and using these abundant stone troughs as planters. Today an authentic, natural trough is a rare and valuable antique.

What is a trough garden? Simply put, it is a container, usually shallow, planted with dwarf plants to make a miniature landscape.

Trough gardens are ideal for the specialist. Virtually any kind of plant can be grown in them, but all the plants in a trough should have the same basic requirements. Members of the American Rock Garden Society have planted troughs with plants of specific areas—the Great Plains, Eastern States and the Siskiyou Mountains. Such a trough garden is designed to represent the landscape of the particular area.

Bulbs, ferns, cacti, succulents and especially dwarf alpines and evergreens do well in trough gardens. One gardener reported that from her experience, most hard-to-grow plants seem to do better in a trough. Tiny dwarf plants that would be lost in a normal-scale landscape are handsomely displayed in a trough.

Why the characteristic size and shape of a trough? Originally they simply imitated the stone sinks that became popular, but the practical aspects have outlived the fashion. A horticultural consultant, Frank Mackaness, notes that: "People have tried troughs of other shapes and dimensions but they keep coming back to the sink size. This is probably because plants require at least the volume of soil that a sink holds . . . . Trough gardens are gaining in popularity, particularly among connoisseurs of choice small plants."

What are they made of? The trough itself is made with a mixture of peat moss, vermiculite, perlite and cement. This material—a good potting soil with cement—has been given the name "hypertufa" because of its resemblance to tufa, a porous rock regarded by knowledgeable gardeners as one of the best media for the roots of alpine plants.

Further characteristics of hypertufa are described by A. James MacPhail of the American Rock Garden Society: "A trough made of hypertufa has many of the attributes of one made from natural stone. The particles of peat distributed within the walls of the container serve to even out the moisture supply available to the roots of the plants. Indeed, should a plant be removed from the container after a year or two, it will be observed that many of the plant's fine feeder roots have attached themselves firmly to the hypertufa surface, a sure sign that they find this material to their liking. In appearance, too, the hypertufa trough resembles natural stone with its strata lines and roughened texture. A newly made trough has an aged appearance, as though it had lain for decades awaiting discovery in some musty recess of an English farmyard."

How to make a trough. A trough is made by molding hypertufa mix into a simple wooden mold. Before the mix is fully dry, the mold is removed and the trough is "antiqued" using a rasp and wire brush. After further drying, several drainage holes are drilled. The step-by-step procedure appears on this page.

The organization most involved with trough gardening is the American Rock Garden Society, 3 Salisbury Lane, Malvern, PA 19355.

Plants for trough gardens are available from nurseries that specialize in dwarf and miniature plants. There is a listing of mail order suppliers on page 109 and 110 of this book.

Trough construction

In many areas troughs can be purchased but many gardeners will want to make their own. Here, adapted from A. James MacPhail of the American Rock Garden Society, are directions for building a trough that is 36 inches long, 20 inches wide and 8 inches deep.

Step 1. Assemble the wooden mold. It consists of an inner and outer form. The space between them determines the thickness of the walls; the space below the bottom of the inner form determines the thickness of the bottom. Walls and bottoms are usually 2 inches thick.

The outer form of 2 by 6 lumber is held together with long wood screws started on the outside of the four corners. The inner form, made with 2 by 4 lumber, is held together with metal "L" brackets screwed into each corner. The connectors between the inner and outer forms maintain proper spacing, although you can judge the spacing by eye.

Step 2. Use a paint brush to apply linseed oil or motor oil to all wooden surfaces that will come in contact with the hypertufa mix. The oil prevents the hypertufa from sticking to the sides of the forms when they are removed. Some oil on your hands is also a good idea.

Step 3. With tin snips or heavy scissors, make the wire reinforcing basket from 1/4-inch hardware cloth. This should be sized to fit the exact center of the walls and bottom of the trough. For a trough with outer dimensions of 36 by 20 by 8 inches, cut the wire 34 inches long, 18 inches wide, and 6 inches deep. Cut this from a single piece of hardware cloth—see photograph—and discard the excess material from the corners. Wire the corners securely together.

Step 4. Place a layer of newspapers on your working surface, preferably a flat wooden floor. Place the outer mold on the newspapers and check it for squareness.

Step 5. Mix the hypertufa ingredients. Use approximately 1 part cement, 1 part sand and 2 parts milled peat moss. The trough will be considerably lighter if vermiculite and perlite (mixed 50/50) are substituted for the sand. A trough this size will require about one bag of cement, and an equal amount of sand (or the mixed perlite/vermiculite) and twice that amount of peat moss. It is better to make two or three batches of this material as the work of filling the mold progresses, rather than mixing it all at one time. Add enough water to make the mix the consistency of cottage cheese.

Step 6. This is an optional step. Mix 1 part cement to 2 parts sand. Add enough water to make a runny mix like heavy soup. Use this in the walls of the trough in thin layers to simulate the random occurrence of natural rock strata.

Step 7. Start casting the mold by filling the bottom of the outer mold to a depth of 1 inch with the mix. Smooth and press the material well into all the corners, using a mason's float or small board.

Step 8. Place the wire reinforcing basket on top of the inch-thick layer, making sure that it is centered from all four sides of the mold.

Step 9. With the basket in place, continue adding to the bottom layer until it is about 2 inches thick. Thus the bottom of the basket will be embedded in the middle of the bottom of the trough. The wire basket is critical to the trough's structural strength.

Step 10. Place the inner mold in position. It will rest on the layer of mix at the bottom of the larger mold. The inner and outer molds should now be at the same height and with a space of 2 inches around each of the four walls remaining to be filled. The sides of the wire basket should reach to within 1 inch of the top of the molds.

Step 11. Fill the walls of the mold. Be sure to force the material into the corners so that no air pockets remain. (Alternatively, add the soupy mix during this stage: see Step 6.)

Step 12. Wait until the trough is semidry. This usually takes about 24 hours but varies with the amount of water used, humidity and the temperature. Begin to remove the mold, the inner one first. Unscrew the four "L" brackets and collapse the mold inwards. Then remove the outer mold, also one board at a time. Be careful with the trough at this point, for it is still very green.

Step 13. After another 24 hours, begin scraping off any humps or ridges where the inner form may have pressed in too deeply. Also, patch any cracks or breaks.

Step 14. Rounding off edges and giving the trough texture is the next step. Depending on the dryness of your trough at this point, you may want to wait another day. Use a rasp and wire brush for texturing.

Step 15. Now leave the trough for at least a week, until it fully hardens. Then "cure" the trough to neutralize the harmful effect of the cement on the plant roots. This is accomplished by filling the trough with water to which about half a teaspoonful of potassium permanganate crystals have been added. Use a paint brush to spread the solution on the outside as well as the inside of the trough. After a few hours, drain the trough and rinse well with cold water.

Step 16. After curing, the trough can be stood on end and drainage holes drilled. Make about 9 holes with a ⅝-inch masonry drill. Wait a few more days and the trough is ready for use.

Planting. The design shown is one of the many possible. Use the native landscape of your area for a model. Dwarf or miniature varieties of many native plants are available from specialist growers. Check "Sources," pages 108 to 111.

Small Space

*What to do with a limited amount of
outdoor garden space. Here are some
common landscape problems and solutions.*

The gardens photographed and illustrated on the following pages will give some idea of the scope of designs that can solve problems in small-space gardens. Each represents only one solution among the many possible. The main point is not to be intimidated by a difficult landscape problem.

Think it through. What do you need—privacy, protection from sun or wind, low maintenance, room for the kids, a hobby area, or a garden for outdoor entertaining? Many gardens need to serve a combination of such uses, and that does add to the challenge. Planning for just one specific kind of garden is much easier, so you might consider first the garden you most need or want.

The photographs throughout these pages are examples. They are personal solutions to the design problems that are always, in some regard, unique. Architecture, the design of surrounding buildings, plays a fundamental role in the success of a garden design. Some gardens are easy to design. Others will require a more prodigious effort. If the job seems beyond your grasp, consult with a professional. You can quickly gather from them simple ideas that may bring to focus the design you need.

As with many problems, the solution to a difficult landscape situation lies primarily in organization. Once your needs and preferences are clearly enumerated, the problem is more than half solved. Use all the materials and ideas available. But remember, the design needs to suit only you and your family.

When space is limited, clutter is more apparent. Tools and toys need a convenient, out-of-sight storage space. If it can be built in, all the better. A successful design is practical as well as attractive.

The function of an entry garden is to provide an obvious, navigable and handsome path to your front door. An attractive entry is one of the best ways to tell your guests "Glad you're here." For some houses, the best plan for the entry may be obvious. For some, it is not. See pages 32 and 33.

Patios are essentially solid surfaced extensions of the home. Patio shapes and situations vary as widely as the homes they complement. If a patio is the total of your garden space, a containerized garden will solve many problems. Vines and creepers can be trained along a fence. Think of a patio as an outdoor living room. See pages 34 to 37.

Sideyards are either shady or blistering hot and are often the most intractable landscape problem facing the homeowner. Espaliered trees or shrubs will fit such a space. Think most of all how you can *use* the space. With shelving, it may be perfect for storage. See pages 38 to 41.

For several good reasons, many people are choosing to live in mobile homes. Based on our investigations, creating a sufficient sense of privacy is one of the outstanding landscape design problem. A trellis covered with a vine is one solution. On pages 42 to 45 are some examples of handsome mobile home landscapes.

For some time there has been a growing interest in what is commonly called "gourmet" food preparation. A kitchen garden is a perfect complement. It's nothing fancy or a fad—just people improving the quality of food they eat. Fresh herbs and vegetables a few steps from the kitchen satisfy this interest. Besides, a kitchen garden is a great time (and money) saver. Pages 46 to 49 have some ideas.

What about shade? Shade is usually too much or too little, depending upon your gardening interests at the moment. What plants grow in shade? How can you add color to shade? Few sensations are more welcome on a hot summer's day than the shade of trees and shrubs. For some problem-solutions, see pages 50 to 53.

This small overgrown garden is a visual treat in an otherwise urbanized landscape. It doesn't take acres of green to counter the effect of an equal amount of concrete and steel —the power of even a few plants is considerable.

Entryways

The most important function of an entryway is to direct visitors to the door of your home. It should accomplish this with a maximum of grace and a minimum of fuss. The design should be simple and in harmony with the style of the house.

Extend the courtesy principle. Consider, first where guests usually park their cars. If they park at the curb, some kind of landing is usually necessary. Don't make them step out into a bed of ivy or juniper ground cover. Very often people will park both in front and in the driveway, so you may want two paths that combine at the main entrance.

If possible, an entrance pathway should be wide enough to be comfortably navigated by two people walking abreast. Depending upon the proportions of the house, a wider path may be best but in any case, try not to make guests approach the door in single file.

The entrance pathway should be interesting but not so convoluted that it is difficult, or worse, dangerous to use. Avoid cracks between boards or stones that could catch heels. Any steps should be low, well lighted, and easy to maneuver.

An entryway that begins with the first step from the car is a courtesy of yours that guests will perceive. It says you care enough about them to make their trip to your front door safe and simple.

Therefore, keep the basic functions of the entry in mind and strive for simplicity in design. Do some research and have a plan. This will avoid two of the most common mistakes: planting a hodgepodge of unrelated plants and overplanting.

Near the end of this book we list some favorite small-space plants. They will give you a good start on your own plant selection. Another Ortho Book, *Garden Construction Know-How*, details the actual building of a variety of entryways.

Design for simplicity with style. Our dress, habits and many other characteristics tell the world who we are. Such statements are best when designed and not accidental. To guests arriving at a home, the entry is the first statement—often the most remembered—about the home and its occupants.

A display of spring-flowering bulbs in containers offers a cheerful welcome to visitors. Plant material changes with the season.

Top right: Gaslight, wrought iron, and a profusion of greenery create a fantasy mood at the entrance to a well-known San Francisco Victorian residence. Right: Brick, laid in a precise basketware pattern, give a well-ordered impression to this contemporary setting.

First Prize, Small-Space Gardening Contest, 1979
Sid and Jean Pidgeon

"My husband Sid built the five heavy planters for the courtyard wall at the front porch two years ago. I replant them each spring and fall.

*"As soon as the summer flowers go—that is the alyssum (*Lobularia maritima*), lobelia, geraniums, marigolds and petunias—I immediately plant the winter bulbs. I use daffodils, narcissus, crocus, tulips and hyacinths. Then in spring as soon as weather permits putting out the new bedding plants, I dig up all the bulbs and transfer them to a holding bed in the back yard to finish off their drying out process. Then after they are fully dried, I dig them, wash and dust them, and store them in mesh bags until fall (all labeled of course). Sincerely, Jean Pidgeon."*

When well planted, enclosed entryways create an air of mystery and anticipation. Abundant greenery and some sunlight keep them from becoming too cave-like.

Patios

Gardens are not just for gardening. They can provide a place to play, cook, eat, meditate, dance or bathe. In fact, there are those who would say that, weather permitting, almost any activity done indoors can be done more pleasantly outdoors. Ancient and not-so-ancient civilizations in inviting climates incorporated some form of indoor/outdoor living in the design of their homes and buildings.

The classic patio, as it has come down to us from the ancient gardens of Egypt and Persia, was a relatively small area surrounded by high walls, often located in an open space at the center of the house. Inside the walls there were paved areas used as walkways. There was a geometric shaped pool at its center to supply the sound of water and a place to grow aquatic plants, and sufficient trees or arbors to create cooling shade. Beds for vegetables, herbs or flowers were laid out geometrically along the walls, or in quadrants around the pool.

The sound of birds and falling water, plants lush from the protected environment, the seclusion of four walls, dappled sun and shade, and the scent of flowers made such a patio an enticing space.

Modern patios can easily recreate this image and, except for the extravagance of the fountain and high walls, the total effect is the product of design and style, not necessarily expense. From the standpoint of conserving water, keeping a garden condensed into a small enclosed area makes good sense in many geographic areas, particularly in areas with arid or Mediterranean climates such as the southwestern United States.

Of course the term patio no longer refers only to a walled-in space. Patios and terraces today are more often thought of as simply outdoor living areas. People and furnishings are as much a consideration as they are inside the house, and both require some type of solid flooring. The material used to pave outdoor areas may be brick, concrete, asphalt, flagstone, tile, precast concrete pavers, or a variety of soft pavings such as bark, stones or crushed gravel. The material you choose depends on how much you want to spend, and how well the material relates the patio's uses to the surrounding garden and to the house.

Aside from wood decking, brick and concrete are probably the two most popular forms of solid garden paving.

Brick would probably rate A+ as a garden paving. It's non-skid and non-glare, comes in colors and sizes that are just right for garden use, can be laid in a variety of

Flagstone has long been a popular paving surface for walkways and patios. It requires considerable skill to install and is comparatively expensive.

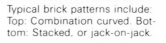
Typical brick patterns include: Top: Combination curved. Bottom: Stacked, or jack-on-jack.

Top: Basketweave. Bottom: Running bond

patterns and combinations, and is ideal for do-it-yourself projects.

The best way to select color and type of brick is to look at what choices are offered at local brick or supply yards. Then order enough to complete the job, figuring 5 normal-size bricks per square foot to allow for some breakage: common bricks are approximately 3¾ inches wide by 2¼ inches thick by 8 inches long. Use "weatherproof" bricks in severe winter climates. Check with the brick dealer for local recommendations.

Bricks usually come in palettes and are often delivered in multiples of 500 although a smaller quantity is available, usually at a slightly higher price. Have them unloaded as near as possible to the work area.

Patterns can be decided upon by laying out bricks in different ways to see what looks and works best (see photographs, page 34). Running bond is simple and well adapted to brick-on-sand. Basketweave leaves a large open joint at one end, so is better used with mortar joints. Stack bond or jack-on-jack can look crooked and are difficult patterns for large areas. Herringbone requires lots of cutting if the edges are to be straight. The variations are infinite, but a simple pattern is usually better than a complex one, for the latter can appear "busy" and is more difficult to lay.

For many people, brick is the first and only choice for garden paving. The way brick combines with green foliage has become something of a garden classic. The standard sized brick is well scaled for small and large areas alike. Brick has become increasingly expensive in recent years, but many homeowners feel that it is worth the extra expense for present enjoyment and future value.

At left, the garden of George Stewart, San Francisco, is one of our favorite small gardens. See the front cover for another view of the same garden.

With the addition of furniture a patio becomes an outdoor room, capable of many functions—dining, cooking, lounging, and entertaining.

Right: The smallest concrete or brick pad can serve as an outdoor escape—if there's room for a chair or two, there's room for enjoyment.

Concrete is practical and versatile. Because there are a great many choices in layouts, color, texture and patterns, a paved surface can bring beauty, along with practicality, to the patio. Working with concrete does require some muscle, but there are ways to minimize the work. You can create the design and do all the grading and forming. Then, if you call in professional people to pour and finish, you'll save some energy and still save money. If you are concerned about a particular finish, buy yourself a sack or two of readymix material and make some stepping stones to practice on before you tackle the big job.

Do-it-yourself Garden Construction Know-How and *How to Design & Build Decks & Patios*, other books in the Ortho series, have complete instructions for installing a wide variety of surfaces. For information on these and other aspects of building a patio, check these resource books.

Making patios into living areas

A patio invites people out from inside the house. Comfortable garden furniture, outdoor dining tables, cooking facilities, and the garden itself all serve to beckon people outdoors. Clusters of different size terra-cotta pots filled with colorful annuals, wooden containers planted with more permanent greenery, cheerful hanging baskets, or a cooling breeze under a shady arbor can make a patio a very livable place.

If you plan to use the patio at night, you will want to add some form of lighting and perhaps heating. The lighting can be as simple as candles placed inside white paper bags partially filled with sand, or as sophisticated as a low voltage electrical lighting system for the entire garden. Low voltage systems are relatively easy to install, especially when done ahead of the construction of the patio. For more information, consult your garden center or electrical shop.

Heat in the garden can be provided with an outdoor fire pit, or one of the relatively new outdoor space heaters that run on propane. If you plan some type of overhead covering, remember that a solid surface such as fiberglass, wood or even canvas will trap much of the heat radiated during the day. If this heat buildup is a problem, plan for some kind of open cover, such as lattice work, lath or widely spaced boards that will allow good ventilation.

Patios

Consider these factors:

Gardens are not just for plants. Some hard surface, such as brick or concrete, makes an outdoor "living room." With the addition of furnishings—chaise, table and benches, barbecue, and sun protection—an inviting outdoor space is created.

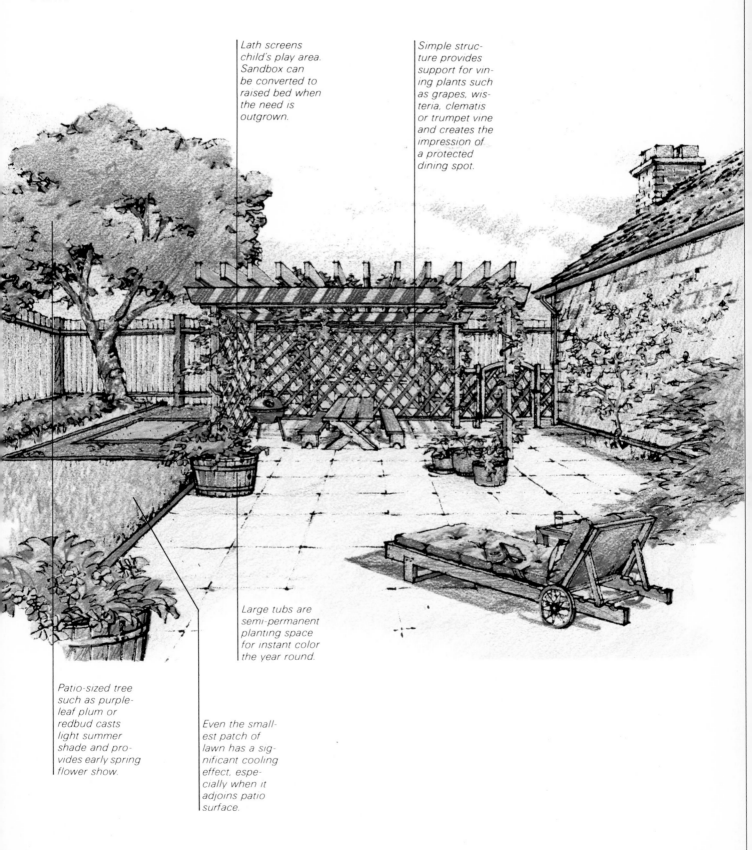

Lath screens child's play area. Sandbox can be converted to raised bed when the need is outgrown.

Simple structure provides support for vining plants such as grapes, wisteria, clematis or trumpet vine and creates the impression of a protected dining spot.

Patio-sized tree such as purple-leaf plum or redbud casts light summer shade and provides early spring flower show.

Large tubs are semi-permanent planting space for instant color the year round.

Even the smallest patch of lawn has a significant cooling effect, especially when it adjoins patio surface.

Sideyards

Sideyards are the hinterlands of most homes. Banished to these long narrow recesses are garbage cans, storage sheds, a drying line or the dog run. Granted, these necessary items have to be put somewhere, but more often than not they're put in the sideyard without much consideration of alternatives.

Anyone who wants maximal gardening in minimal space should not overlook the potential of the sideyard just because it is long and narrow.

With an addition of a simple arbor between house and fence, and pavement, gravel or bark underfoot, the sideyard can become a sheltered colonnade for growing shade-loving flowers in hanging baskets and pots. The word "arbor" most often conjures up images of grape or wisteria vines, but there are attractive substitutes such as clematis, honeysuckle, climbing roses, or the rampant-growing passion flower vine. With clusters of hanging

Formerly a wasted space, the shaded sideyard at left now makes a lush and ideal environment for several kinds of ferns and rhododendrons. Baby's tears fill in around plants and narrow brick walk. Above, the cool and casual design of this sideyard makes the best possible reading spot during a summer hot spell. Right, the dense growing shrubs help insulate the house and make an attractive border.

A simple design solution such as shown above is often the most effective. The large size bark chips match the fence color, and are inexpensive and simple to spread. Medium sized shrubs that won't outgrow the space are chosen.

At top, a bonsai specialist has made full use of a sideyard for tool and supply storage as well as display. Note the overhead structure that provides shade and shelter.
Above, this viewing garden is an enclosed section of a sideyard. It is covered and usually left open to the living room.

39

baskets filled with impatiens, begonias, coleus or other colorful plants, the sideyard viewed from inside the house can be a very pleasant place.

More often than not, one side of the house is used as a pathway from the front to the back of the lot. If you often find yourself taking loads of rubbish, garden or pool supplies back and forth, make sure the walkway is comfortably wide and paved with a surface that's easy to travel, such as concrete or asphalt. Consider, too, the width of a gate. If you're going to pass through it often with a wheelbarrow, be sure to make it wide enough so that you don't scrape your knuckles.

If an easy passageway is what you're after, it's a good idea to keep plantings flat against the wall or fence. Espaliered fruit or ornamental trees and shrubs (see page 00) can be kept to within 6 to 8 inches from the fence. For more information about training espaliered trees and shrubs, see Ortho's *All About Growing Fruits & Berries.* Not all plantings against a vertical surface need to be espaliered fruit or ornamental trees and shrubs (see page 22) can be kept to within 6 to 8 inches from the fence. For more information about training espaliered trees and tha, evergreen pear (*Pyrus kawakamii*) and xylosma can be trained into a very narrow hedge—less than 12 inches thick.

If you want to screen out the neighboring view and still leave room for unobstructed passage, consider planting fast-growing, tall shrubs such as *Pittosporum eugenoides* or Carolina laurel in a row next to the fence. Prune the shrubs to direct the growth upward, eventually baring the trunk to the top of the fence. At that point, let the plants branch out, and within a few years you'll have a dense screen and still have room to use the walkway.

If you do not need a clear passageway, the options are more diverse. A winding path creates more esthetic interest than a straight one, and provides interesting planting spaces on either side.

The sideyard can be an ideal place for a potting shed built against the house or fence. The addition of a small lath shade overhead can make the workspace even more pleasant. In many gardens shelves can be attached to the fence for displaying potted plants.

Sideyards can be productive, too. Because berry vines are not the most attractive element in a landscape, putting rows of vines in a long narrow area makes sense and keeps them shielded from view. Perennial vegetables such as artichokes, rhubarb and asparagus would all do well segregated in an area next to the house.

Raised beds can make a narrow yard into a productive vegetable garden. In the award-winning garden in Philadelphia (this page) the grade up the hill, the brick pathways, and the random placement of the raised beds make this particular garden interesting and inviting. If there is a kitchen door entering onto the sideyard, it might be the place for a kitchen garden of herbs and salad foods—see pages 46 to 49.

Award of Merit, Small-Space Gardening Contest, 1979
John Webster

"I live in the Federal Hill district in a typical row house that overlooks downtown Baltimore. It had been something of a run-down area but is experiencing a dramatic revival. This year twenty homes and gardens in my neighborhood (mine included) have been chosen to be part of the annual Maryland House and Garden Tour. It's really this spirit of revival that has inspired me to experiment and try to apply some of my own ideas.

"My own background includes horticultural training but not in design. Two years ago I began experimenting in the empty lot behind my house just to see what could be done. At that time garden design was only a hobby.

"I don't have any simple all-encompassing theory of what makes a landscape design work, but there are some things I've learned.

"Most importantly I've learned how to include the elements of the neighborhood, even the distant city if visible, into the plan. For instance, the growing beds in my yard are aligned lengthwise with neighborhood houses visible from my backyard. Also I've used my neighbor's mimosa (Albizia julibrissin) as a focal point of my garden. Many visitors have commented that my garden looks much bigger than it really is and I'm sure the reason is the way neighborhood features are a part of the design.

"The other idea of mine is to use vegetables and fruit plants with ornamental characteristics. I normally grow broccoli, tomatoes, cabbage, eggplant, celery, many kinds of lettuce, carrots, rhubarb, asparagus, blueberries, strawberries and green peppers. These food plants are as important to the attractive look of my yard as typical landscape shrubs. Sincerely, John Webster."

Award of Merit winner in the sideyard category was John Webster of Baltimore. His use of the narrow area was attractive and productive.

Sideyards

Consider these factors:

It is a space small enough to overlook and yet large enough to make good use of. Its narrow shape demands imaginative design.

Microclimate conditions are often intense. Modification is often necessary.

Most gardens need space for utilitarian use: Garbage cans, drying lines, potting areas and other storage facilities are in this category. "Utilitarian" doesn't necessarily mean unattractive.

Simple lattice overheads, using fence uprights provides cooling relief from south facing exposure.

Shelves, attached directly to the fence, make good use of seldom used space.

Potting area with hinged bins for soil storage could also double as garbage can disguise.

Curved planting spaces create non-linear pathway—proves the most pleasing path between two points is not necessarily a straight line.

SMALL SPACE

Mobile Homes

Most mobile home owners don't want the responsibilities or inconveniences of an ordinary "stationary" house. However, they do want the warmth and personality of a fine residential home, along with the conveniences, ease of upkeep, as well as the privacy that few other kinds of homes can match.

Sometimes the move to a mobile home means a reduction in available garden space for gardeners used to much more. Retired couples accustomed to a much larger home often experience this. In contrast, a young family may have more garden space than they had at their first small apartment. In either case, mobile homes offer some specific landscape challenges.

Landscaping mobile homes presents some unique considerations. Screening for privacy and noise reduction are a major objective. This gardener, right, relied on the tried-and-true qualities of roses and low-growing junipers for beauty and service. Below, tulips add interest to an otherwise evergreen landscape.

Privacy. A valued premium anywhere, privacy is often difficult to obtain in a mobile home park. Sometimes local ordinances specify the maximum number of units per acre. How these units are arranged on the property dramatically affects your sense of privacy. Mobile homes arranged in clusters instead of rows can open up much more green space and common areas without drastically reducing the number of homes.

The sense of privacy is also enhanced by the lay of the land. Berms and banks and small hills add contours that are attractive and also reduce noise. Of course, a well-landscaped mobile home park increases the beauty of the area and can make it much more pleasant to live in.

In the absence of such features, mobile home residents usually think of some kind of fencing for privacy. Chain link fences are strong but often not attractive. They do have the advantage of being easy for many climbing and vining plants to attach to, but until completely covered, they offer only a see-through kind of privacy. Several varieties of easy-to-build wood fences are fully described in the Ortho Book entitled *Do-It-Yourself Garden Construction Know-How*.

There are several varieties of patios, decks and carports that can be adapted to mobile homes (see the sample landscape plan, page 45). But be sure to check local building codes before getting started with add-ons. In most places, codes prevent structure such as these from actually touching the mobile home itself.

Simple decks and screens increase the available living space and expand landscape possibilities. Trees, shrubs and flowers in containers can be arranged. Fast-growing annual vines in containers will, in the course of one summer, completely cover a lath screen. Or a little kitchen garden may suit your purposes better.

The vegetable gardener at top found room for vegetable favorites along a common pathway. Attractive lattice-work above encloses patio creating privacy but still allows open feeling.

Individuality. Many mobile home residents express interest in increasing the individuality of their homes. It's a consideration not unique to mobile home owners, but in some cases their need is very apparent. Extensively landscaped parks or those with the homes arranged in the cluster fashion have the least need. Landscaping alone masks structural sameness. As trees and shrubs grow, the sharp lines of the trailers fade from sight.

Individuality is primarily created by developing a plan for your outdoor space that enables you to make the most of it. As your yard becomes organized, it will develop over the years to reflect your personality and style. Whatever is most important to you in your yard will eventually dominate the landscape.

Top: Customized deck for hot tubbing provides comfort and privacy in a minimum of space. Middle: Bronze colored hopseed bush, *Dodonaea viscosa* 'Purpurea' is tough, fast growing and dense—all the requirements of a good screen plant.

Plants reduce noise. Noise is, by definition, disagreeable. All of us need some refuge from it. That mobile homes have thin walls is no secret—it's the main way their weight is kept low enough for mobility. Depending upon the location of your mobile home and the overall arrangement of the park, the intensity and type of noise you receive varies. But for many mobile home residents, most of the sounds they hear are noises, not pleasures. Landscaping is a partial solution to the noise problem.

Shrubs and trees are effective sound mufflers. They don't block all sound but do reduce its intensity. Plants slow the travel of sound waves much as they do wind when they are used as a windbreak.

The most effective sound mufflers among plants are dense-growing plants with soft foliage. The hollies (*Ilex* species) are attractive broad leafed evergreens that are excellent foundation shrubs. Several varieties of the hollies qualify as good sound screens.

Conifers such as the yews (*Taxus* species) and the hemlocks (*Tsuga* species) are dense but will require some maintenance. The hemlocks, especially, are fast growing and usually require shearing to keep them in shape.

Very easy-care but also hardy shrubs are the buckthorns (*Rhamnus* species). They are partly deciduous in very cold areas. These plants and some others in our list of small-space shrubs (page 96) are a good starting point for planning your quieted mobile home garden. You'll also want to check with a local nursery for other screening shrubs that like your climate. Don't forget that plants with rustling leaves may help mask unattractive sounds.

Bottom: The handsome landscaping and permanent features of this mobile home all contribute to its "homey" feel.

Mobile homes

Consider these factors:

Confined space leaves little opportunity for privacy. Noise—from either street or neighbors—is a consideration when landscaping the mobile home. Close placement of units can create an overall uniformity which only landscaping can correct.

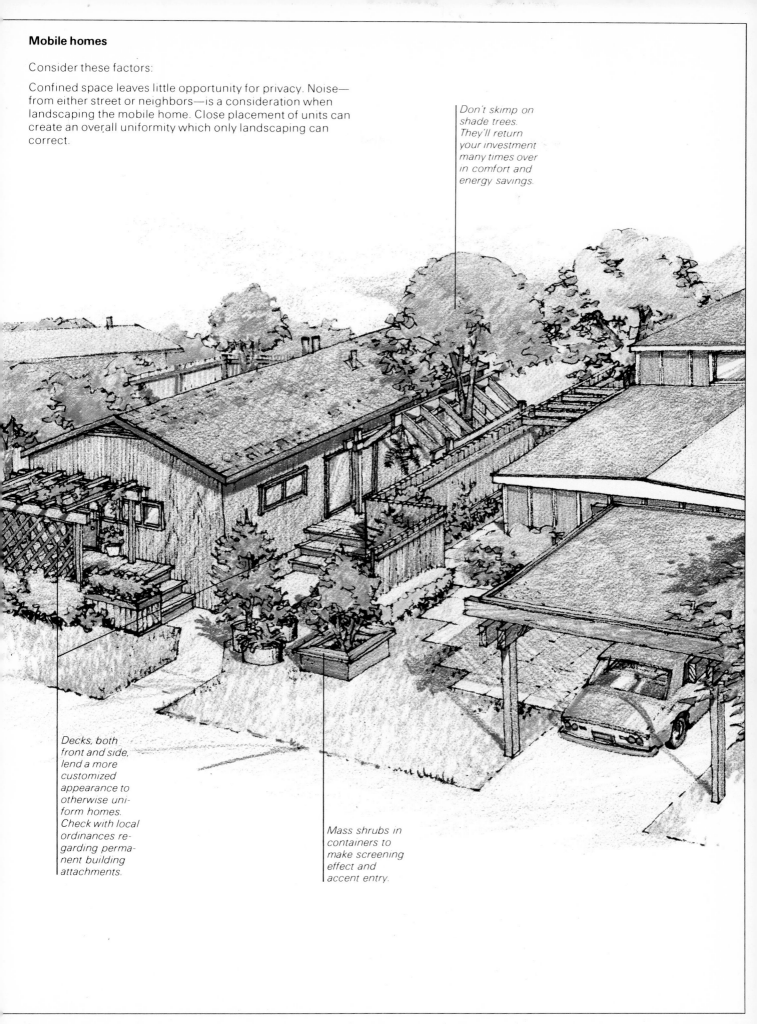

Don't skimp on shade trees. They'll return your investment many times over in comfort and energy savings.

Decks, both front and side, lend a more customized appearance to otherwise uniform homes. Check with local ordinances regarding permanent building attachments.

Mass shrubs in containers to make screening effect and accent entry.

SMALL SPACE

Kitchen Gardens

Kitchen gardens are among the most basic and common kinds of garden. Certainly they are the most useful. Most gardens, as they are or will develop, are combinations of many kinds of plants. For our purposes, a kitchen garden means one with herbs and vegetables that are used on a daily basis. If possible, a kitchen garden should be close to the kitchen, to save steps.

Why a garden just for the kitchen?

The answer is well known but it bears repeating: fresh herbs and vegetables taste better. Not only is the flavor more pungent and distinctive, but the nutritional value is often higher in food that is eaten immediately after it is harvested. Increased awareness of food quality and tastes often accompanies the development of gardening skills.

Convenience and cost savings are other important reasons for a kitchen garden. Why get in the car and drive to a market to buy a bit of lettuce or a few sprigs of parsley? With containers of such plants on the patio or balcony, the need in the kitchen is satisfied with a few steps.

Keep in mind that most kitchen plants are not delicate or hard to grow. On the contrary, most start readily from seed and are not particular. The ease with which these herbs and vegetables are grown adds to the good sense of starting a kitchen garden.

Another good reason for a kitchen garden is to provide hard-to-find gourmet vegetables such as the globe artichoke, its relative the cardoon, and endive. Such plants are often easier to grow than to find in the markets.

How to get started. Decide on the plants you want to start with and where they will go If you're lucky enough to have some soil near the kitchen, you may want to use that space. If it's not a good, friable loam, add plenty of organic matter—compost, ground bark or peat moss—to loosen it.

Maybe all of your kitchen garden will be in containers or planters. The local nursery will have many kinds, or you can make containers from the plans found in other Ortho Books. Fill the containers with a good lightweight soil mix as described on pages 18 to 19.

Most kitchen plants are available as young plants. That's the easiest way to start. A wider choice of varieties and unusual vegetables can be found either on the nursery seed racks or from mail order suppliers.

Above, an arm's reach away—herbs go from container to pot in minimum time for maximum flavor. A kitchen garden needn't be simply utilitarian. The two gardens at left combine the best of the edible and the ornamental.

For kitchen gardens

Here are suggestions for herbs and vegetables that, growing near a kitchen door, will make preparing food more pleasurable and eating it a delight. Many other plants could qualify for a "kitchen garden." After all, such a garden should suit personal taste. There are many publications that deal with kitchen plants in depth. See, for instance, Ortho's *The World of Herbs & Spices* and *All About Vegetables*.

Herbs

Basil. This popular herb is grown in gardens today both as a seasoning for hundreds of dishes and as a beauty in flower borders and in containers.

There are two basic kinds of basil—sweet basil (*Ocimum basilicum*) and bush basil (*O. minimum*). Sweet basil is an annual that grows 1 to 2 feet in height and has leaves that look creased down the center. This is the basil most often grown for cooking.

Basil is easy to grow. Seeds germinate readily in spring as soon as the ground warms. Give it regular watering and full sun—but some shade is okay. Go easy on fertilizer—too much will reduce flavor. Basil grows well in containers and under fluorescent lights.

Left: Classic herb garden is laid out in circular pattern. Top: Herbs for a spaghetti sauce grow in old olive oil containers. Above: In a deep container, you can grow carrots.

Cut leaves as you need them, or cut the branches and gather in bunches for drying. Basil can also be frozen.

Chives. This is a perennial plant that grows in clumps of slim leaves to heights rarely beyond 10 inches. Lavender flowers cover the plants in late spring or early summer.

Chives are easily grown from seed and will do well on a windowsill. Most nurseries have small plants available. Chives are adaptable. They'll grow in shade and light soil but do best in full sun and humus-rich, moist earth. They grow well under fluorescent lights.

Snipped off close to the ground, chives will rapidly renew themselves. Unless clipped regularly (about three times per season), they may become rather tough and chewy.

Cilantro. This plant has different names depending upon the use it's put to. For its seeds, the name is "coriander"; for Chinese cooking, its parsley look makes it "Chinese parsley"; but for Mexican dishes, the name is "cilantro."

The plant is a fast-growing annual. Its height is generally 1 to 2 feet. It has oval leaves with serrated edges on the main stems.

Cilantro is easy to grow. It likes sun or filtered shade and well-drained soil. Sow the seeds in place in early spring and thin until plants are 7 to 10 inches apart. The plants adapt well to container culture.

Start picking the leaves for use when the plants are 4 to 6 inches high. For the summer months, the supply will be bountiful. Store the leaves in the refrigerator in a glass of water covered with plastic. The leaves can also be chopped and frozen, or dried whole and later ground as you would other leafy herbs.

Garlic. In much of the world's cooking, this is the one indispensable herb. To an Italian or French cook, it's hard to imagine anyone conducting a kitchen in proper fashion without it.

Two types of garlic are available. One is the type you buy at the market, a bulb containing about ten small cloves; the other is the so-called elephant garlic, which is about six times larger and may weigh a full pound. Elephant garlic has a slightly milder flavor than the standard kind.

Where the ground does not freeze, the bulbs are set out in the late fall to get the maximum size. In cold winter areas garlic is planted in spring. The bulb does not grow as big with spring planting. In either case, garlic likes full sun and rich soil.

Water garlic deeply but infrequently, for excess water will discolor the white or pinkish sheath that surrounds the cloves. Harvest when the tops are beginning to dry out and fall over. They are dried in the sun and when the bulbs are dry, the tops can be braided into strings or tied in bunches and hung in a cool, dry well-ventilated place.

Oregano. This is an attractive shrublike plant that grows to 2 or 2½ feet in height. Related to sweet marjoram, it has a somewhat sharper flavor.

Oregano will flourish in well-drained garden soil. Give it full sun and plenty of water. It adapts well to containers. Trim it occasionally, both to harvest the leaves and shape the plant. Under fluorescent lights, simply shear back the top of the plant several inches when it reaches too close to the light.

Start from seeds or established plants. Thin the seedlings to give each plant about a foot each way. Plants may need replacement after three years or so if they become too woody.

Gather fresh leaves when you need them. They can be dried, or freeze them in a plastic bag.

Parsley. Three main types of parsley are grown in this country—curled, plain leafed and turnip rooted. The Moss Curled type is very popular. It has very dark green and deeply curled leaves. There are other strains of Moss Curled called Triple and Extra-Triple Curled.

Italian parsley has uncurled leaves that are dark and glossy green.

Parsley is a biennial that is usually treated as an annual. It is not difficult to raise from seed, and transplants are available from nurseries.

This plant prefers some shade and a moderately rich, moist soil. Thin to 6 to 8 inches apart. It is easy to grow in containers.

Pick the leaves as you need them or harvest in bunches to dry or freeze.

Don't forget that parsley can be used as a highly decorative edging for a flower bed, or as an attractive pot plant indoors with light from a bright window or from fluorescent tubes.

Rosemary. This is one of the most important kitchen herbs. Without it a lamb roast is nearly impossible for some people to enjoy.

Rosemary is a not-quite-winter hardy evergreen which has several varieties that grow between 2 and 6 feet in height. In mild climate areas, it can make an excellent hedge and can also be used as a ground cover or trained to grow against a wall. Ground-hugging types spill over the edge of containers most attractively.

Cold climate gardeners should grow rosemary in movable containers so it can winter over in a

It's easy to plan for succession of lettuce crops when the lettuce is grown in a container. Simply plant individual containers at intervals that correspond to your use.

frost-free but cool place.

Rosemary grows in almost any soil provided it is well drained. It should receive plenty of direct sunlight but not much water. It can also be grown indoors in containers. The plants need frequent tip pinching to direct growth. Use these pinchings for flavoring.

Dry the sprigs in bunches or dry the leaves in plastic bags to enjoy the delightful flavor and fragrance of this herb all year.

Sage. The familiar garden sage (*Salvia officinalis*) is a hardy perennial that grows to about 2 feet tall. Its long and oval gray green leaves are coarse in texture. Violet blue flowers appear on tall spikes in summer. Garden sage is universally available as either seeds or plants.

Sage thrives in poor soil if it is well drained. It needs full sun but comparatively little water. Garden sage is easily started from seed, from stem cuttings or by dividing established clumps in the spring.

Pineapple sage (*Salvia elegans*) is a tender perennial. Except in mild winter areas, it is best grown in a pot or tub so that it can be brought to a frost-free location during cold weather.

Pick sage leaves for kitchen use before, during or after bloom. Cut back the flowering stems after the blooms are gone. The leaves can be stored dried or frozen, or whole branches can be hung upside down and dried.

Tarragon. There are a number of varieties of tarragon. Best known in this country is French tarragon; Russian tarragon is less familiar to most gardeners.

French tarragon is a perennial that spreads by rhizomes. Its slender, dark green leaves are distinctly aromatic. Its flowers are small, tightly clustered, and whitish green. The plant grows to between 1 and 2 feet high and is decorative when used in a flower border or potted. It does not bear seeds and must be propagated from cuttings or by division.

Russian tarragon looks much like its French cousin but has greener, rougher leaves, does bear seeds, and is less pungent in flavor.

Tarragon requires well-drained soil and a warm, mostly sunny location. As with many herbs, the best flavor comes from plants produced in rather lean soil. In cold climates, the roots should be protected by a covering of mulch. Small root pieces can be potted in summer and set out the following spring. Established plants should be divided and replanted every 3 or 4 years.

For best flavor, gather the leafy stems just before or just as the flower buds begin to show. Hang the stems upside down to dry.

Thyme. The most flavorful variety of thyme to grow for seasoning is common thyme (*Thymus vulgaris*). It is a shrublike perennial with small, gray green leaves and lilac colored flowers. It will grow to a height of 6 to 12 inches. The many different varieties of creeping thyme make excellent ground covers in a sunny spot, and their leaves are good for seasoning.

Thyme should have lots of sun and light, well-drained, fairly dry soil. It can be started from seed or propagated from cuttings. Thin the seedling plants, leaving 8 to 12 inches between them. Thyme is a shrubby plant that can become woody if neglected, so it should be kept well clipped. Snip off 2 or 3 inches at a time when the tips are growing vigorously during late spring or early summer. After a few years, the plant may show too much woody stem. The clump can then be divided and reset in fresh soil.

Thyme leaves may be dried in the oven. Store dried leaves in an airtight container or freeze them.

Vegetables

There is much more about vegetables later in this book, on pages 74 to 79. That is where you'll find details about container culture. Here we want to draw your attention to some kitchen garden favorites.

Beets. Easy to grow, this is a two-in-one vegetable—the greens are as edible as the root.

Beets germinate readily from seed even in cool soil. The plants themselves will tolerate light freezes. Thin the seedlings early and plant every two or three weeks for a continuous beet harvest. Beets will grow well in partial shade. Try the baby size varieties.

Carrots. Sow seeds directly where the plants are to grow as soon as the soil can be worked in spring. Look especially for the short varieties. They are very sweet, a perfect size for hors d'oeuvres, and rarely available in markets.

Lettuce. There are four types of lettuce and dozens of varieties. The trick is to choose the variety that fits the season in your locality.

Crisphead (also known as iceberg lettuce) is the kind displayed in markets. It's not impossible to grow in the home garden but is exacting in its requirements.

Butterhead types make loosely folded heads. They are rarely grown commercially because they bruise and tear easily. This is a good one for the home garden. Look for the 'Summer Bibb' and 'Buttercrunch' varieties. 'Tom Thumb' is a miniature small enough to serve the head intact.

Leaf lettuces grow most openly. There are many variations in leaf color and leaf shape available. 'Grand Rapids,' 'Prizehead' and 'Bronzeleaf' are good early varieties. 'Slobolt,' 'Salad Bowl' and 'Green Ice' are more heat-resistant.

Cos or Romaine lettuce grows upright to 8 or 9 inches. 'Dark Green Cos' and 'Paris Island Cos' are widely adapted.

Lettuce has a limited root system and occupies the soil for a relatively short time. Therefore, fertilizing and watering are both important. If the growth of a young plant is checked by lack of nutrients or water, it never fully recovers. For best growth, add fertilizers to the soil before planting and water regularly.

Spinach. Spinach is a cool weather crop and is not difficult to grow if you have the stretch of weather it requires. It is surprisingly hardy but will flower with increasing temperature and length of day. In mild winter areas, spinach is a late fall and winter crop. In colder climates, plant spinach in early spring. For the kitchen garden, it's easiest to start with transplants.

Tomatoes. Look to the small-fruit varieties that grow well in containers. They are the best bet for a kitchen garden. You may have favorite varieties but we recommend you try 'Salad Top' or a similar one. It will grow well in a 6 or 8-inch pot but stays less than a foot tall. Its fruits are an inch in diameter. 'Small Fry' is a cherry-type and a 1970 All-America Selection. Others to consider are 'CB-City Best,' 'Gardener's Delight,' 'Pixie Hybrid' and 'Stakeless.' 'Tumblin' Tom' is well adapted to hanging baskets.

If you buy transplants from a nursery, look for bushy, stocky plants. When you plant, plant deep—up to the first set of leaves.

Kitchen gardens

Consider these factors:

Builders of condominiums and townhouse developments often provide small but useful pockets for gardening. We found this illustrated gardening space a common situation. If located near the kitchen, we'd make good use of space for vegetables and herbs. If you've ever had to drive to the market for a garlic clove, you know the value of a kitchen garden.

There's always room for a container or two that will provide a quick clipping of your favorite herbs.

Exterior walls, two stories in height, can be an awesome surface to work with. Espaliers, either formal or freeform, soften the harsh effect and provide crop as well.

Where garden space is limited, raised terrace gardening increases efficiency. Compound raised beds of varying depths provide ideal conditions for vegetables having different root requirements. When filled with a light-weight soil mix, it's practically a vegetable factory.

49

Shade

Shade can be evergreen or shade can be colorful, whether on a front porch, north-facing balcony (see page 60) or patio. But shade is a problem because it reduces the choice of plants available for your garden. Most landscape plants need plenty of sunlight. But there are still many plants that will do well in shade.

Shade defined

Shade is a word that must be carefully weighed by the individual gardener. Shade is one thing when summer days are consistently sunny and bright, and quite another when the garden receives only 50 percent of the possible sunshine.

There is also the type of shade that exists beneath a dense evergreen shrub or tree, where essentially no light penetrates. That type of shade never supports plants.

The word shade never stands alone in the language of gardening. There is partial shade, half shade, filtered shade, filtered sun, shadow shade, light shade, dappled sunlight and deep shade.

The blessing of shade. Shade from a wide branching tree, or from a vine covering a pergola, or from overhanging eaves can be a real comfort on hot summer days.

In landscaping a small space for human comfort, hedges and fences—added for privacy and wind control—increase the amount of shaded area. As trees grow and increase their spread, they further reduce the light that reaches the ground.

For many gardens the time comes when an area of "full sun" is hard to find. It's usually then that the gardener starts thinking of shade in terms of plant growth.

How much light. All of the words that modify descriptions of light—filtered, partial, full—are expressions of light intensity. Full sunlight at noon delivers 8,000 to 10,000 foot-candles of light. Early morning and evening light are in the 1,000 foot-candle range. Cloudy days often decrease the intensity of the light striking the garden to below 1,000 foot-candles.

Many plants create their own shade problem. A tomato plant growing in full sunlight may receive 10,000 foot-candles at the top level of leaves and less than 200 foot-candles at the lowest level. That's one reason the lowest leaves yellow and drop.

More shade or less shade?

Since shade is often a blessing, you may want more of it. Conversely, you may want to reduce it for the sake of some plants.

As plants grow, the shade they cast is naturally increased. But you can quickly add more shade to the garden with a trellis, arbor, pergola and similar structures. They may be permanent or lightweight, seasonal arrangements. Annual vines can be trained to grow over them to add to the shade that can be realized in one season. Shade cloth used by commercial growers is long lasting and can be very attractive. It is available in several widths from garden centers.

When there is already too much shade in the garden, you can selectively thin the trees and shrubs that block most of the light. The additional light may not seem significant to your eye, but it may be just the amount needed by the lawn or ground cover beneath. If for some reason you don't want to or can't prune to add enough light for plants to grow, use fir bark, wood chips or a similar kind of mulch as a ground cover. Heavy mulches are attractive, keep weeds down and blend with the plantings.

Star performers in shade

Ferns and many colorful foliaged plants have a natural place in the shade. But when you start looking for trees, shrubs, annuals or perennials that will add color and texture to shade, the list of candidates is shortened.

Most gardeners take the advice that a certain plant "does well in shade" too literally. Generally, if the amount of sunlight is increased to the maximum that the leaves will tolerate, the plant will deliver maximum bloom or growth. Equally true is the fact that the sun-produced bloom will last longer when protected from the direct sunlight. Remember, almost any plant will remain bushy and strong for weeks (and bloom profusely) if it is grown in full sun and then shifted to the shade garden. In this instance, containerized plants again prove useful.

Trees. Small trees that are native "understory" trees of the forest are shade tolerant. Across most of the continent, the Japanese maple (*Acer palmatum*) is one of the very best small trees for shady gardens. It's a favorite of many people, and hundreds of varieties are available. The closely related vine maple (*A. circinatum*) is sometimes a tree and sometimes a shrub, but is very handsome and takes considerable shade.

Flowering dogwoods (*Cornus florida*) are also native understory trees that tolerate shade but boast a brilliant flower show in spring. Plant them in acid soil.

For mild climates, several of the *Podocarpus* species make a good choice for shady gardens. Sometimes called "yew pine," they have a very strong oriental character. They grow well in containers, can be espaliered or trained into a hedge.

Shrubs. The range of shrubs that grow well in shade is relatively wide. In warm climates, one of the best is the Japanese laurel (*Aucuba japonica*). It is reliable in even the deepest shade. Somewhat hardier is the classic fragrant sarcococca (*Sarcococca ruscifolia*). It is another of the best low-growing shrubs for shade.

Many of the acid lovers are good shrubs for shade. Plants such as azaleas and rhododendrons (*Rhododendron* species), winter daphne (*Daphne odora*), lily-of-the-valley bush (*Pieris japonica*), and skimmia (*Skimmia japonica*) all do well along shaded entryways, along walks and in containers.

Winter creeper (*Euonymus fortunei*) is hardy and a real workhorse in shade gardens. Use it as a shrub, ground cover or vine. Make it into a hedge or train it flat against a wall.

Perennials. Here the plant list broadens significantly. These include many of the best shade-tolerant ground covers as well as flowering perennials. The large bellflower or *Campanula* family includes many shade plants. Most nurseries regularly have three or four varieties on hand. Barrenwort (*Epimedium* species) are deciduous but that is no loss in areas of heavy winter snow. They are hardy and in summer make a uniform cover about a foot high in deep shade.

Ferns, of course, are great shade plants. The Japanese painted fern (*Athyrium goeringianum* 'Pictum') needs wind protection but is otherwise hardy and an attractive shade plant. Wood ferns (*Dryopteris* species) are larger and more dramatic, but also hardy shade lovers.

The plantain lilies (*Hosta* species) should be singled out for mention. There are many species and all make interesting shade plants by virtue of their large leaves. They are deciduous but quite hardy. They take lots of water and need protection against snails and slugs.

On pages 90 to 107, more shade plants are noted. Starting with these suggestions, you can consult your local nursery to widen the choice of shade plants that will do well in your climate.

Opposite: A gallery of shade-lovers, clockwise from top left: wild ginger (*Asarum caudatum*), clivia, old-fashioned violets (*Viola odorata*), impatiens, primroses (*Primula polyantha*), woodsorrel (*Oxalis oregana*), and golden vancouveria (*Vancouveria chrysantha*). Right: Mature oaks make dappled shade perfect for both outdoor dining and shade-loving plants. The irridescent colors are the flowers of tuberous begonias.

Color in shade

Here is a chart that will help you bring touches of brilliance to dark places in your garden.

Name of Plant	Type	Remarks
Begonia, fibrous rooted *Begonia semperflorens*	Perennial used as an annual	Flowers in red, white, pink. Leaves are deep waxy green or bronzy red.
Edging lobelia *Lobelia erinus*	Annual	Use dwarf compact kinds in wide shallow pots and trailing type in hanging baskets.
Flossflower *Ageratum houstonianum*	Annual	Compact multi-branch plant, 5 to 12 inches high. White, pink or blue flowers. An excellent dwarf variety is 'Blue Monk.'
Forget-me-not *Myosotis sylvatica*	Annual	Look for dwarf kinds. Brings hues of clear blue into the shade border. Grow in a wide shallow pot.
Miniature pansy *Viola tricolor hortensis*	Perennial grown as an annual	Use for spring and summer color in cool climates.
Nicotiana	Perennial grown as an annual	Flowers of the older kinds open in the evening and are very fragrant. Newer introductions flower in daytime but are not as fragrant.
Painted leaves *Coleus*	Perennial grown as an annual	Prized for brilliantly colored leaves. Use outdoors in summer and as houseplant anytime. Color not as vivid in shade.
Patience plant *Impatiens walleriana*	Perennial grown as an annual	Bright scarlet, pink, orange, red, rose or white flowers 1 to 2 inches across. Dwarfs and semidwarfs are available. Plant in partial shade.
Sapphire flower *Browallia speciosa* 'Major'	Annual	Brilliant blue flowers like a giant lobelia. Blooms all spring and summer until frost.
Scarlet sage *Salvia splendens*	Perennial	Often listed as plant for full sun but does well in semi-shade.

Vegetables in the shade

Where there is no space with full sun, the general rule to use in deciding where to locate vegetables is as follows: All vegetables grown for their fruits or seeds—such as corn, tomatoes, squash, pumpkin, cucumbers, eggplants and peppers—should have the sunniest spots. Vegetables grown for their leaves or roots—such as beets, cabbage, carrots, chives, kale, leeks, lettuce, green onions, parsley, radishes and Swiss chard—can be grown in partial shade.

First Prize, Small-Space Gardening Contest, 1979
Marie Tietjens

"One of the many hobbies my husband and I have is gardening. Our first garden after we were married was a windowbox on the outside windowsill of a fifth floor apartment in New York City. Our current garden began to develop about 11 years ago when our boys were no longer at home.

"Each year, Max would develop a particular area. Our garden is sort of a miniature arboretum. We have many different kinds of plants.

"My main interest is in azalea propagation by cuttings which I do under glass jars. I have had tremendous success with not only this method for rooting cuttings, but I have also grown hybrid rhododendrons and azaleas from seed. It's a most fascinating hobby!

"We have many individuals, garden groups, school children, and senior citizens visit our garden. We like nothing better than to show it off. Most of all, we like walking along the garden paths every day of the year and discussing how we will improve the garden for next year. Sincerely, Marie Tietjens."

First prize winner Marie Tietjens utilizes this shady corner of her garden for propagation of azaleas. Top left, Marie prepares the cutting to the proper length. Top right, the leaves are cut in half to reduce water-using leaf surface. The jar cover keeps humidity high enough to promote rooting.

Shade gardens

Consider these factors:

City gardens, by the nature of their surroundings, are often extreme in their conditions. Many older homes have sufficient gardening space, but the available sunlight is blocked by surrounding buildings. In such cases, careful plant selection is a must. Check for plants in the shade-loving section of your nursery. Adding color to the garden can be a problem, but plants can be brought to bud in full sun, and then brought into the shade to bloom.

The all-green shade garden is a common one. Color, concentrated in containers, adds sparkle and interest. Good candidates include impatiens and fibrous begonias.

Selective pruning of surrounding trees and tall shrubs will add substantial light. Trees with fall color can be especially dramatic in the shade.

No Space

You have no outdoor garden space. What about the roof? A balcony? The deck? Indoors? A windowbox? A garden can be any place and any size.

What makes a garden? We think it is the intent of the gardener. That is why the size of the garden makes no difference. A "garden" can be in a teacup. The methods and tools used by the gardener do not define the garden. Expertise is irrelevant to the character of a garden: about any gardening subject there's always someone who "knows" more. The purpose of this chapter is to show real gardens in unlikely places and encourage you to start your own.

Do you have a flat rooftop that's not being used? If you think roofs are only fit for vents, wires and air conditioners, what follows will change your mind. Turn the page to see some very beautiful gardens on rooftops. Look at what our Grand Prize winner, Libbie Stewart, did with her Philadelphia rooftop (see page 58).

Balconies are familiar components of city apartments, condominiums, townhouses and penthouses. So many kinds of gardens can be made on balconies. We've seen some with lawns, shrubbery and trees recalling a suburban landscape. Some balconies have complete food gardens: dwarf fruit trees and vegetables in containers. Some balcony gardens are elegantly designed and make a delightful entertaining area.

A deck can be a great problem-solver in modern landscape design. Notwithstanding the variety of problems decks solve (especially in areas of uneven terrain), they function to combine the comforts of indoor living with the naturalness and openness of the outdoors. You can emphasize this transition with a lean-to greenhouse. A deck would be barren without a few plants in containers. If your deck adjoins the kitchen, as many do, you'll want a planter for some herbs, lettuce and carrots (see pages 46 to 49). On page 67 is a landscape plan rich in ideas for a deck.

Indoor gardening has changed. There was a time growers couldn't keep up with the demand for such plants as Boston ferns and grape ivy in 6-inch pots. Now the demand is for larger plants and more thoughtfully planned indoor landscapes, or what we call "house gardens." Plants carefully chosen, grown and arranged is the style today. Artificial lighting greatly expands the possible locations. Many plants are easily brought from seed through bloom without a flash of natural sunlight. Two Award-of-Merit winners with indoor garden rooms are featured.

Want the last word on windowboxes? See pages 72 and 73. So commonplace it's overlooked, a simple windowbox filled with trailing geraniums can add charm and a sense of caring to a home. A neighborhood dressed up with only windowboxes undergoes a definite character improvement.

Plant lists and projects for "no-space" gardeners are included in the last chapter of this book, beginning on page 89.

The "Notebook" is an informal discussion of the many plants that are useful in small gardens. It starts on page 90 with our recommendations regarding some of the best trees for small gardens. There are several lists for quick reference that will help find a tree for a specific use or situation. A similar pattern is followed on the topics of shrubs, ground covers, vines, perennials and annuals. Use the chapter as a guide to build a basic plant list.

Perhaps the most inventive gardeners of all are the gardeners who are faced with no outdoor space at all. We feature their gardens in this chapter.

It's hard to believe this garden was created on a balcony several stories up. Brick paving, permanent planter with large tree, and plenty of seasonal color make this small space an oasis.

Rooftops

Rooftops offer an unlikely garden possibility. Maybe the roof is the last place you'd consider, and gardening there may seriously challenge your perseverance. But when a few problems are solved, a garden on the roof may well become the most memorable one you'll ever make.

Many apartment buildings have both flat roofs and open basements. The basement is perfect for a fluorescent light system to start seedlings destined for the roof. Make it a cooperative venture with others in the building. Such a gardening cycle could remake the character of the building as well as add fresh produce to the table.

Maybe you've occasionally used your rooftop for sunbathing. Especially where buildings are tall or close together, roofs will receive more sunlight and give more privacy than patios and backyards. Bring up chairs for friends, an umbrella for shade and some potted plants for color, and your roof garden is begun.

Two of our award-winning gardens are on rooftops. Following are the experiences of these winners and other rooftop gardeners.

The determined gardener is not put off by the difficulties inherent in rooftop gardening. In any given city, rooftops represent acres of unused space.

Before the roof is a garden. If you are thinking of some full-scale gardening on your roof, here are some tips.

Most likely the roof doesn't leak. If it did, the last rainy season would surely have been a test. But a leak caused by rain in the natural course of things and one caused by roof gardening are different. You don't want to feel responsible for any damage. Gardening will expose some parts of the roof to almost constant soaking as you water your garden there. That's why it's essential to inspect the roof thoroughly for watertightness.

Check with the planning department of your city to be sure there are no ordinances prohibiting roof gardening. Otherwise, all your planning and planting may be wasted.

Be sure you have permission of the building's owners. They will want assurances of safety. They may also help you bring water, electricity and other conveniences to the roof if such utilities are not there already. They are usually more familiar with the building and how such jobs can be most easily done.

Finally, check the support structure of the roof. Some rooftops will be substantial and others less so. Local building codes specify the minimum load a roof must support.

Problems of rooftop gardens

Gardens on rooftops are unique in many ways and you may encounter problems you didn't expect. Here are some potential problems.

Wind. Like balconies, rooftops are exposed. They lack the protection of surrounding trees, shrubs and buildings. Further, wind often gains velocity as it is funneled down the steel and concrete canyons of our cities.

Wind will have two important effects on your roof garden. You may find that more plants need the support of a stake. This may be particularly true of fast-growing annuals and vegetables that would normally not require a stake. For them just a short, finger-sized piece of redwood or bamboo on the windward side of the plant is sufficient.

Wind also affects watering practice. Wind can, in a sense, pull water out of the plants and so increase their need of it. Plants vary in the ability to tolerate the drying effects of wind. In some cases, a burlap or similar wind shield is necessary. To make a windy rooftop more comfortable for yourself, you'll need some kind of windbreak too.

Sun. Sun isn't usually a problem. In fact, plenty of sun is one of the advantages of rooftop gardens. But some kind of shade to retreat into will make conditions much more congenial for you. Every garden needs an area where the gardeners can withdraw and survey their good work.

Air pollution. This is an unfortunate characteristic of some city gardens. Here are two suggestions for dealing with it.

Keep in mind that the plant leaves are collecting dust and debris from the air (filtering the atmosphere, in effect) and that soot blocks sunlight. Wash the leaves as frequently as possible with a fine spray.

More insidiously, some plants are damaged by invisible chemical components of smog. Petunias are so sensitive to such pollutants and they can be used as indicator plants. If their leaves show a silvery flecking and no insects are present, they are probably being damaged by chemicals in the air. Japanese maples, some orchids and rhododendrons are also sensitive but to a lesser degree. Food plants such as apple, beans, citrus, grapes and even tomatoes have shown either damage or slowed growth because of air pollution.

Weight. There are two important points here. Plan on using a lightweight soil mix. It will be about 60 percent lighter than an equivalent amount of garden soil. And consider how you will carry the soil to the roof (which is not an easy route in some cases), as well as the ability of the roof to support weight (see page 62).

If you have any lingering doubts about the strength of the roof, arrange the heaviest containers and planters around the edge. That's closest to the walls where strength is greatest.

Water. We've assumed thus far that you have a conveniently located water faucet. If you're not so lucky, make arrangements for putting in a pipe or hose from the nearest outlet. Don't even consider lugging water to the roof in a bucket, unless the garden is very small or all succulents.

Tar paper. Roofs surfaced with tar paper need protection against foot traffic. Tar paper is easily damaged by the leg of a chair or the edge of a container. Wooden decking on a flat roof is relatively simple to install. It will add immeasurably to the appearance of the rooftop and protect the roof's surface.

Award of Merit, Small-Space Gardening Contest, 1979
Laura Bentley

"In 1974 when my garden was bulldozed to make room for a parking lot, I felt so badly that I even resigned from the garden club of which I had been a member for 25 years. Truthfully, I felt that since I no longer had a garden, then what had I to offer? Love for my flowers had been a part of my life; and my husband, knowing this, said he would make it up to me. He decided to buy me a greenhouse. Now living in an apartment over the top of the market with the whole back yard black-topped, we wondered where we would put it. Where else but the ROOF! Ideally the greenhouse would face south but since this was not possible we settled for the next best, which is east. In the meantime, along with my other house plants, I began collecting orchids. I joined the Orchid Society and my collection grew from our inter-society auctions. By the fall of 1975 the greenhouse was completed.

"At first we had only a few plants but now our collection has passed the 400 mark. We have about 14 species of orchids as well as a beautiful pink bougainvillia that has grown to tree proportions. We also have a night blooming cereus (Cereus peruvianus) that last year had 45 blooms and 14 at one time. There are also many ferns, palms, a bird-of-paradise and some cacti.

"Since my outdoor garden was gone, I tried to make the greenhouse look like an indoor exotic garden. The entry to it is through a sliding glass door from my living room, under a trellis on which hangs our phalanopsis onto a walkway. Small stones under the benches keep the required humidity at a suitable level and there is even a sink and small potting bench at the end.

"Being up high there is no shade at all so we must move all the plants into a lath house constructed on the north side porch where they summer. My husband Fred will be installing a cooling unit for the next season. Sincerely, Laura (and Fred) Bentley."

At left, note how condominium rooftop utilizes tailored hedge plants to define space and create privacy. Right and below, Laura Bentley's rooftop greenhouse.

Grand Prize, Small-Space Gardening Contest, 1979.
Libbie Lovett Stewart

"I have been gardening on my roof (deck) for about 8 years. My main interest is to see what will grow. I try different things each year. I've grown sweet peas, violas, bulbs, watercress, vegetables (I grow these in an 8 by 16 foot plot in a nearby community garden), Tithonia (Mexican sunflower), and dahlias to name a few.

"I have two large strawberry jars, one filled with alpine strawberries and the other with perennial herbs. I leave them on the deck over winter covered by large clear plastic bags. By March there are blooms on the berry plants.

"I have a small cold frame and experiment to see what I can grow over winter in it. It helps grow both early and late lettuce.

"My greenhouse is vented automatically, reducing heat build-up. I almost never have to use supplemental heat due to the southern exposure and heat from the attached wall. I use the greenhouse to start seeds and root cuttings (but I do buy many fresh plants from the nursery).

"Because I cannot see the deck in the winter, I have no evergreens or other shrubbery. Presently I have two rose trees, two rose bushes and six miniature roses.

"My deck never looks the same because I try new plants and shift them around each year.

"At first I depended almost entirely on annuals but have been gradually introducing more and more perennials. I look for perennials that bloom for at least two months.

"A large tree grows at the end of my rooftop-deck. This gives me some shade and makes for a gentle breeze. During summer, I keep hard-to-grow plants, that need lots of moisture and shade, in the greenhouse.

"I stay plenty busy as a free-lance graphic designer. That means that many times my plants are neglected but they don't seem to mind too much! Sincerely, Libbie Lovett Stewart."

The judges felt Libbie's rooftop-deck garden met all the criteria of a grand-prize winning, small-space garden. The aesthetic qualities are clearly apparent just from the photographs on these pages, but her garden neither was installed nor is maintained by professionals.

Mildred Mathias, Executive Director of the AABGA and Director of the University of California at Los Angeles Botanical Garden, introduced Libbie's garden to the other judges. She thought it was "especially imaginative" and went on to describe many of the aforementioned special features. Later, Bob Montgomery, Director of the John J. Tyler Arboretum in Philadelphia, said: "I think Libbie's garden should be singled out as a really outstanding example. It's clearly superior to all the others." Fred Widmoyer, Chairman of the Department of Horticulture at New Mexico State University, summarized for all the judges: "The important thing is that Libbie Stewart has created a work of art utilizing plants and architectural features."

Libbie Lovett Stewart, winner of the Grand Prize award. Small-Space Gardening Contest, 1979. Libbie is a busy graphic designer and avid gardener. The combination of her talents and interests is evidenced by the photographs on these pages. Excluding some assistance with the actual construction of the deck, credit for the results is wholly her own.
For another view of Libbie's garden, see the back cover of this book.

Far left: The rooftop deck was constructed largely on the ground in individual units. These sections were then hoisted to the roof and situated in place. Results included minimum rooftop work and interesting visual pattern. Note also the small table—its scale is perfect for this tiny garden. Left: A favorite perennial of Libbie's is the button chrysanthemum pictured close-up at left. Tiny flowers are usual and flowering season is long. Top right: Libbie's garden viewed from direction opposite to far left. Note the small greenhouse for starting seeds. A small door designed to allow rooftop access was enlarged and now serves as frequently used garden entry. Right: Petunias and geraniums are two of the annuals that Libbie frequently uses.

Balconies

Balconies for gardens may be smaller than 30 square feet or as large as a small suburban backyard. There are no standard dimensions. Most balconies, however, do share certain characteristics.

Balconies need wind protection. Elevated from the ground, they are more exposed to cold winds. This problem is often extreme at the upper reaches of a modern highrise.

At ground level, there are trees, shrubs and nearby buildings to slow down the wind. Wind will pass over the top of a windbreak, leaving essentially dead air below and slowed air for a good distance ahead, depending on the height of the windbreak.

Experiments have shown that houses protected by a windbreak use 10 to 25 percent less heating fuel in winter.

If summertime prevailing winds are a problem on your balcony, consider building some kind of screen to break them. Glass or fiberglass will not block the light from plants, but the framework will have to be fairly sturdy. A lath screen is easy to make and can double as a trellis.

If your balcony landscape includes plants intended to stay out year round, the wind will exacerbate the climatic demands made on them. Wind coupled with either heat or cold is the most severe test of a plant.

Help your plants by providing a modified environment—shade and wind protection—as well as good culture. Otherwise, ask at the nursery for the toughest plants. The Russian olive (*Elaeagnus angustifolia*), tamarisk (especially *Tamarix aphyla*), and several of the pines—especially the Scotch pine (*Pinus sylvestris*)—are some examples. Hardy shrubs would include forsythia *(Forsythia ovata)*, several of the hollies (*Ilex* species), and the cotoneasters. See pages 89 to 107 or your local nursery for more details.

"My balcony faces north. It never gets direct sun." The direction your balcony faces in relation to the sun will determine to a large extent the kinds of plants that will grow and the general landscape of your balcony. An easy mistake is to assume that because a plant grows well on your neighbor's balcony, it will on yours. The two balconies could be facing opposite directions.

A north-facing balcony will receive less direct sunlight than any other. The shade problem may be further compounded by the overhang of eaves or a balcony above.

If shade is your problem, ask at your local nursery for the most shade-tolerant plants. Japanese laurel (*Aucuba japonica*) is one of the best plants for deep shade. Another large shrub you might consider is luster-leaf holly (*Ilex latifolia*), which is also a good espalier specimen. Where they can be grown, tree ferns are excellent. Some other trees and shrubs for shade include the Japanese maple (*Acer palmatum*) and podocarpus.

Left and right, a city balcony of approximately 60 square feet. We found it as shown left, saw the possibilities, and decided to experiment. The results are shown at right. The owner reported, "The change was more dramatic than even I expected. My guests and I would naturally gravitate to the landscaped balcony. It became the most used room of the house!"

First Prize, Small-Space Gardening Contest, 1979.
Stephen Tollefson

"This balcony is a space of about 4 by 7 feet. It is visible from several rooms in the apartment so it occurred to me to try to do something with it. Originally it was the front landing of this 1890 Victorian building when it was still a single family home. Through many—mostly ill-advised—remodelings, it has become the crazy-Moorish balcony it is today. I get to it from a sitting room through low French windows.

"The floor was originally covered with asphalt roll roofing. Over this I laid a half-inch layer of potting soil and set bricks in a basketweave pattern. I packed soil between the bricks and planted baby tears around the edges.

"I have a total of 35 container plants on the floor and sidewall, on small shelves, and hung from the walls and archway.

"A cast-concrete lion's head fountain with a small electric pump makes cool sounds on warm days and helps mask traffic noise from the busy street below. A wind chime also helps mask unwanted noise.

"I use a 100-watt floodlight mounted above the inside of the arch for night lighting. It shines like moonlight into the adjoining rooms.

"The balcony faces east and provides light conditions ranging from very shady to semi-sunny.

"The baby tears catches much of the drainage water from the container plants. Some drippings onto the steps below does occur but the neighbors don't seem to mind. Sincerely, Stephen Tollefson."

Bob Montgomery, Director of the John J. Tyler Arboretum in Philadelphia introduced Stephen's entry to the other judges. He said, "Judging from these slides (Stephen sent 35mm transparencies of his balcony with the entry) this is a most beautiful garden. I'm not that familiar with San Francisco but if somebody were to show me these slides I would have said San Francisco was the location. I wouldn't be surprised at all to see this garden in House Beautiful. I think it is a serious candidate for a top award." Later, Bob said that when he first looked at the pictures, he felt that such a balcony would be "a good place to have a cup of coffee in the morning."

Left and above, the thirty square foot balcony of First Prize winner, Stephen Tollefson. We think you can see what was meant by judge Bob Montgomery (see above) when he said, "It looks like a perfect spot for a morning cup of coffee."

"My balcony faces west. On hot afternoons it's like an oven." Balconies facing west absorb the sun's direct rays from midafternoon until evening. Here you will need shade structures for at least a portion of the balcony, and heat-resistant plants. Dwarf fruit trees might need pampering but will produce on a west-facing balcony better than any other. Bamboos are another good choice here. In no-frost climates, the colorful bougainvillea will thrive in the reflected heat of a west balcony. Train it against a wall or let it drape over the edge. Xylosma and oleander are two very tough, heat-tolerant container plants; so are several of the cotoneasters and junipers.

What about watering? There are two problems here: getting the water to the balcony and then having somewhere for it to drain. If your balcony garden consists of only a few pots, the problem is easy to solve. A common watering can filled in the kitchen will probably be adequate. The amount of drainage water will be minimal.

But if you are a balcony farmer, you've most likely discovered the lack of an outdoor faucet for a hose. Balconies equipped with them are rare. But many kitchen faucets have threads, intended for a faucet aerator, on which a hose adapter will fit.

If you have a portable dishwasher, you're familiar with the easy snap-on fixture used for connecting with the kitchen faucet. These can be obtained from plumbing supply houses and adapted for a watering hose.

Drainage is a problem, especially if the water drips onto the downstairs neighbor's balcony. It's a good idea to check this out before you have any problem. If you do, the simplest solution is a drainage pan under each container.

What about weight? Building codes typically specify that a balcony must be able to support 60 pounds per square foot. Designed to that standard, a 5 by 10 foot balcony would safely support 3,000 pounds, the weight of about 20 people.

Lightweight soil mixes are up to 60 percent lighter than garden soil when fully wet, so save a considerable amount of weight. Of course, the weight of garden soils varies but most are 30 to 50 percent heavier than an equivalent quantity of water. A cubic foot of water weighs 62 pounds, so a cubic foot of soil is anywhere between 70 and 100 pounds. A peat moss and perlite soil mix at full water capacity weighs about 34 pounds per cubic foot. A cubic foot of soil will fill 20 to 22 one-gallon containers or 35 to 40 six-inch pots.

Above: Balcony garden thrives 37 floors above the city of Manhattan, NY. See pages 82 and 83 for other views of the same garden. Left: The tiny balcony of one of our editors. The tree-azalea makes an ideal accent in early spring. A chair and a few simple annuals for color complete the setting.

Balcony

Consider these factors:

Wind: Balconies are less protected by trees and neighboring homes. A highrise balcony is especially exposed. For both people and plants, some wind protection is usually necessary.

Exposure: North is heavily shaded and due west is baked by the afternoon sun. Plant selection must vary accordingly.

Water: Most balconies don't have outdoor faucets. A hose from an inside tap is often necessary. Find out where and how the water will drain.

Weight: Check with your builder or landlord. Typical codes specify a balcony be able to support a minimum of 60 pounds per square foot.

Balconies in normal space high-rise buildings have distinct microclimates depending on the exposure of the balcony.

Prevailing winds don't have to make a balcony uninhabitable. See text for suggestions on how to use baffles or screens.

Under normal circumstances. South-facing balconies are warmest. North. coldest. East. morning sun: West. afternoon sun. Lattice work provides vertical growing space as well as a sun screen.

NO SPACE

Decks

The wide wooden porches and verandas common to homes of an earlier time are probably the precursors of contemporary wooden decks. Today's deck occupies a unique place in the design of residential properties: it doesn't belong entirely to the house, nor entirely to the garden. Inherent in a deck is the feeling of indoor/outdoor living, pleasantly obscuring the distinction between house and garden. Architects and garden designers are quick to use decks of all sizes to enhance outdoor living.

Homes on hillside lots are often the first to acquire an open deck. Level outdoor space can be created in midair with a wooden deck as a logical extension of the house. With the increased use of larger areas of glass, including sliding glass doors, architects, designers and homeowners found that outdoor decks, level with the interior floor space, created a feeling of openness and spaciousness which previously had been impossible to achieve. With the recognition of these special qualities, decks have come into their own.

Top: To avoid disturbing existing tree, hole is made in new deck. As well as providing shade, the tree becomes an integral design element of the deck. Above: For the food gardener, there is always room for a few tomatoes in containers.

Top: Small deck appears to float in the landscape, providing a level spot for sun bathers. Above: Extremely narrow lot makes good use of two decks on different levels.

Planning your deck

One of the best qualities of decks is that their construction is within the range of anyone who can use a hammer and saw. In the northern and mountain states you might want to consult a professional designer to consider snow loads as part of the design. Building permits are usually required, so get one in the beginning to avoid problems later. Some building departments consider a wood deck to be the same as an interior floor and insist on an 18-inch crawl space below the deck. If this is the case where you live, it represents the one advantage that if you ever do change the deck into an actual room, your construction is nearly halfway complete. Always grade the area below the deck so that the water drains away from the house.

Wood is subject to deterioration and damage by dry rot and insect attacks, so it's crucial to select the correct type of wood, preservative treatment, and construction technique. If this is done, wood can be as permanent as many other paving materials. Wood used as outdoor flooring also needs to resist warping, checking and cracking, be reasonably free of splinters, and be strong enough to withstand the load and type of wear it will receive. Rougher textures are usually best for both appearance and safety; finished planks sometimes become slippery when wet.

One simple technique for building a deck is to lay 2 by 4 or 4 by 4 stringers right on the existing grade and nail planks on top. This is a good temporary construction that can be dismantled for winter storage or moved to a different location. The stringers should be treated or naturally decay-resistant wood, but the decking will last many years even if not treated. Brushing or pouring preservative on the stringers and the bottom side of the planks may help slow down deterioration.

Orientation to sun and wind is of primary importance in selecting the best location for your deck. A north or east placement, preferably with a cooling breeze, is best for a warm weather climate. If you live where every available ray of sunshine is greeted with delight, a south or west orientation will trap the heat and sunlight, and cold winds are usually excluded. Convenience to the kitchen or living room, and view and privacy are other factors that may influence the placement of an outdoor living area. Don't overlook sideyards or the front of the house when there is enough space.

Small balcony-deck provides room for an abundance of foliage and flowers. The view from indoors is appealing and inviting.

If you are planning to use your deck for gardening, perhaps you can design for special places to hold a variety of containers or utilize the raised bed idea with a cap on the sides to provide extra seating as well as ease in gardening.

If you have a tree right where you want a deck, don't cut down the tree—build around it. You will have built-in shade and a unique feature to your deck. The pictures on this page show one example of this.

For help in developing the right design for your deck, see Ortho's book, *How to Design & Build Decks & Patios*.

Special problems

If you are working with a house that faces in the "wrong" direction, you can compensate with a trellis or shade tree. A deciduous tree can provide shade in the summer and let the sun warm you in the winter. With the addition of some simple supports, you can create an arbor over part or all of your deck, providing naturally filtered sunlight to any portion of it that you choose.

If your deck is raised a couple of feet or more off the ground, and you have other houses close by, you may find that you are looking at your neighbors and your neighbors are looking at you. This problem can be solved by adding a fence or screen on one side of the deck, as we did in the sample plan (page 67). Train plants along your fence or trellis and you will have a living wall of decorative or food-productive plants.

If your deck provides a sweeping view that you do not want to obstruct, you may want to keep your deck garden very simple. Consider some elegant, small topiaries and clusters of colorful plants in a number of places. Perhaps some bonsai would blend harmoniously with the scenery immediately beyond.

Whatever the size of your deck or the nature of the neighboring environment, there are countless ways to make it a wonderfully pleasant outdoor room. The plan and photos on these pages can help stimulate ideas that will best suit your own needs and desires.

Above: Contoured deck fits into landscape with a natural feel. If your garden is more formal in appearance, consider using a geometric deck.

Right: A simple deck of 2 by 6's and railroad ties provide up-close access to a colorful corner of the garden.

Decks

Consider these factors:

Decks create outdoor living space where a hillside or uneven terrain would preclude use. A deck can be landscaped or "furnished" and become as comfortable as any living or play room. Small containerized gardens can flourish on a deck.

Deck built at same level as interior floor space has the effect of expanding the room, creating an inside/outside flow.

Planter boxes, raised to eye level soften the effect of a fence built for privacy. Especially effective when planted with trailing plants.

Pots filled with seasonal color spark the scene.

With the addition of pillows, wide steps double as seating space.

Open-bottomed, built-in containers allow shade-making trees to grow to their full size. They become a focal point of this deck garden.

House Gardens

Times have changed and house plants have given way to house gardens. Most house gardeners have either large and dramatic specimens indoors and talk about their indoor landscape, or have complete indoor gardens of a certain type.

The life expectancy of plants growing indoors is up. Indoor gardeners and nursery personnel are constantly learning more about what plants will survive. Skylights, new kinds of indoor plant-light equipment and various kinds of watering gauges help here too.

Most importantly, we've learned that what's good for plants benefits people too. Healthy plants indicate a healthy environment.

Here is a review and update on the most pertinent aspects of growing plants indoors. Suggestions are made of plants to try, and the proven ideas include two award-winning house gardens.

Imagine an equation of plant growth: plant + light + soil + water + nutrients + proper climate = plant growth. For the typical indoor plant, light is the one factor most often in short supply. Learn to see the symptoms of too low a light level. First is simply lack of growth. A common mistake is to equate no growth with a need for fertilizer. A plant suffering from too little fertilizer will have stopped growing more suddenly and be a paler green. If the problem is low light, growth will have been slowing for a long time; lower, more shaded leaves will wither and drop off.

Fertilizing a plant in a low-light situation may compound the problem by increasing the salt level in the soil.

There are natural differences in the tolerance of plants to low light levels. If a plant is native to the lowest tier of a tropical rain forest, too *much* light will burn its leaves. Other plants will need full exposure to the sun.

Acclimatized plants. Many of the most popular indoor plants are very adaptable to different amounts of light.

That's what makes them useful. They include such plants as schefflera (*Brassaia actinophylla*) and weeping fig (*Ficus benjamina*). They can adapt to full sun or considerable shade.

The key word is adapt. A weeping fig grown in full sun and moved to a dark corner will likely not survive. At the least, most of the "sun" leaves will fall—a startling thing to see—and be replaced eventually by "shade" leaves. There is a difference between these sun and shade leaves. In the weeping fig, sun leaves are a lighter shade of green and slightly stiffer to the touch. If you have a fairly dark corner for an indoor tree, choose one with succulent, dark green leaves.

Reputable growers are now adapting—or as they say, "acclimatizing"—their plants before delivery to nurseries.

Soil for house gardens. Most indoor plants are in containers, which alone necessitates a light, air-holding soil mix. Further, many indoor plants are native to tropical areas where they grow in almost pure leaf-litter. Second to insufficient light, indoor plants suffer most from soil that contains too little air and, conversely, too much water.

Plants such as Boston fern (*Nephrolepis exaltata* 'Bostoniensis') and prayer plant (*Maranta leuconeura*) have fibrous roots that will quickly suffocate in a waterlogged, airless soil. Both are native to very light soil of almost pure leaf mold. (Unfortunately, pure leaf mold makes a poor soil in a container.) Other plants such as dumb cane (*Dieffenbachia* species) have relatively thick, fleshy roots that will rot in waterlogged soil.

The soil-mix basics for container plants (pages 16 to 19) also work for indoor gardens. Indoors, all the elements of growth are in more critical balance, so it makes good sense to have the best soil possible.

When only a little soil is needed, it's best to buy a commercially prepared mix. These vary widely in quality. If the mix you buy has a predominance of fine particles, it may not hold enough air. Amend it with perlite (which is also available in inexpensive, small bags). Start with about three-fourths soil mix and one-fourth perlite.

Watering. It is a cliché that more indoor plants die of too much rather than too little water—but true. Fast-growing healthy plants are easy to water properly. That's one important reason it makes sense to start with a healthy plant in a good location and in the right kind of soil.

Plants that are growing slowly because it's winter or because they are in a dark corner should be watered less. When light is dim, and growth slow, all cultural operations are more critical.

What is the right time to water? There is no simple rule. Watch the plant. Is the color and physical quality of the leaves right? Scratch the soil at least a half-inch below the surface to judge its dampness. With experience, you'll be able to correlate symptoms and needs.

Sometimes the rootball will dry completely and not

Formal solarium with small pool allows sufficient light for plants and makes the room an enclosed, year round garden.

readily absorb water. Usually the root mass slightly and water runs off the top, down the sides of the container and out the drainage holes. In such situations, use a wetting agent to reduce the surface tension of the water. A wetting agent made for plant use is best but in an emergency, a few drops of liquid detergent in the water will help.

Don't use softened water on plants. The sodium in it is hard on soils and may be toxic to some plants.

When to fertilize. The important point about fertilizing is that it's necessary *when* the plant is growing, not to *make* the plant grow. A plant with ideal greenhouse conditions will normally need three to four times as much fertilizer as the same plant could tolerate in a home. That is because in a greenhouse, plants will grow that much faster. Feed your plants as they grow.

Fertilizers are available in many forms. There are water-soluble pellets, powders and liquids; dry tablets and sticks to insert in the soil; and time-release pellets. Whatever kind you choose, read the label first and follow the directions. Soil should be moist before fertilizer is added.

Temperature. Most indoor plants grow best at daytime temperatures of 65° to 75° F (18° to 24° C). Nighttime temperatures should drop at least 10 degrees Fahrenheit to between 55° and 65° F (13° to 18° C). This temperature drop slows the metabolic machinery of the plant, preventing it from needing more stored energy than it has.

To draw a comparison: the light a plant receives during the day is the fuel, and temperature is the throttle. Temperatures too high relative to the light available during the day will make the plant work too fast.

Be watchful of plants close to windows. Direct sun pouring through can heat the plant to the point of burning it. On cold nights the plant can freeze. At night, put a piece of cardboard between the plants and the window. Also, keep the plants out of direct drafts of cold air.

Good plants that can take freezing blasts of air when a door opens are the paper plant (*Fatsia japonica*), the *Mon-*

stera deliciosa and house-blooming mock orange (*Pittosporum tobira*).

Humidity. The relative humidity inside a home, especially in winter, can be as low as 5 percent. A typical indoor plant struggles to maintain about 40 percent humidity around its leaves. As humidity drops, the plant releases more water vapor from its leaves. It can and often does happen that the plant releases more water to the air than its roots can take up. At that point, leaf edges turn brown and the plant may die.

One of the best ways to increase the humidity around plants is setting them on a pebble tray. Keep the water level in the tray below the top of the pebbles. The pebbles facilitate evaporation of the water, which adds a considerable amount of vapor to the air around the plants. The tray also catches the excess after watering.

Beyond this simple technique, a variety of mechanical humidifiers is available, from small portables to the types built into the home heating system.

Keep track of the humidity in your house with a humidity gauge or "hygrometer." Many types are available, and cost very little.

Man-made sunlight. Artificial lights have greatly expanded the variety of plants and the places they can be grown indoors. Plants can grow and bloom where artificial light is the sole light source. There are incandescent "plant-growth" lamps, fluorescent tubes of various types including high-output kinds, combination incandescent-mercury vapor lamps, and high-intensity discharge lamps (abbreviated HID).

The HID lamps are expensive but just one can illuminate a 4 by 8 foot area. Recently, a HID lamp compatible with standard home wiring has become available (see Sources).

A combination incandescent-mercury vapor lamp is marketed under the name Wonderlite. This type fits a standard light bulb socket but provides growth-promoting benefits far superior to ordinary incandescent bulbs. At a distance of 3 feet, several kinds of indoor plants, such as African violets, will flower with only this lamp as a light source.

Fluorescent light remains the standard for most indoor light gardens. Many special kinds are available for specific plants, but a combination warm-white and cool-white is best for most plants because the actual light output is higher. Keep the bulbs within 8 to 10 inches of the tops of the plants unless you're using high-output tubes, which can be 3 or 4 feet from the plants. Use 20 to 40 watts per square foot of area to be illuminated, and leave the lights on between 10 and 18 hours a day.

The blue-coated incandescent plant-growth lamps are a good source of supplemental light. But the spectrum and quantity of light they emit is not adequate as a sole source of light.

Contemporary indoor garden features open portions of rooftop allowing rain to fall on plants below.

Plants for special indoor situations

There is virtually an endless number of plants that can succeed indoors. It is nearly impossible to categorize them all or to give general advice. From a plant's point of view, an east exposure in one house may be the same as a north exposure in another.

If you don't mind moving plants around, such experimentation is one of the best ways to discover what will grow and where. As a starting point, here are three lists of plants for three different indoor landscaping situations:

Top: Traditional garden/sun room provides high light intensity and protected environment for indoor specimens. Above: Desk-top light garden filled with herbs represents a most compact form of an indoor garden. Right: indoor stone planter has skylight overhead to provide foliage plants with ample light.

For a sun porch. The average sun porch receives a maximum amount of winter light—at least 5 hours a day. Most sun porches are unheated but, because they are attached to the house, stay above 50°F even in winter. Some good plants for such a situation are:

Abutilon megapotamicum	Trailing abutilon
Bougainvillea x *buttiana*	Bougainvillea
Cactus species	Cactus
Campanula species	Campanula
Citrus species	Citrus
Exacum affine	Persian violet
Felicia amelloides	Blue daisy
Fuchsia x *hybrida*	Fuchsia
Jasminum polyanthum	Jasmine
Osmanthus fragrans	Sweet olive
Primula species	Primrose
Streptocarpus x *hybridus*	Cape primrose
Tropaeolum majus	Nasturtium

For dark corners. These are some of the plants very tolerant of low light levels. Fertilize and water plants in dark corners much more sparingly. Occasionally, bring them into stronger light (but not direct sun) to let them build up more food reserves.

Aglaonema species	Chinese evergreen
Aspidistra elatior	Barroom plant
Chamaedorea erumpens	Bamboo palm
Cissus species	Grape ivy
Crassula argentea	Jade plant
Cyperus alternifolius	Umbrella palm
Epipremnum aureum	Pothos, devil's ivy
Ficus elastica	Rubber tree
Monstera deliciosa	split-leaf philodendron
Philodendron species	Philodendron
Ptychosperma macarthurii	Macarthur palm
Rhapis excelsa	Lady palm
Rumohra adiantiformis	Leather fern
Spathiphyllum species	Anthurium
Syngonium podophyllum	Nephthytis, arrow-head vine

When there's little water. Many people enjoy being surrounded by plants in the home but haven't the time to give the daily care some require. Maybe you travel frequently, leaving your plants for a few days or weeks. The plants listed below are well known for their ability to survive days, weeks and sometimes months without water.

Aloe species	Aloe
Beaucarnea recurvata	Elephant-foot tree
Bromelia species	Bromeliad
Cactus species	Cactus
Chamaedorea erumpens	Bamboo palm
Crassula argentea	Jade plant
Cycas species	Sago palm
Euphorbia milii	Crown-of-thorns
Gasteria species	Mother-in-law's tongue
Haworthia species	Star cactus
Portulacaria afra	Elephant bush
Sansevieria trifasciata	Snake plant

Award of Merit, Small-Space Gardening Contest, 1979
Kathleen Buchanan

"My garden is really two gardens. From the first to the last frost, panels are installed around my deck that convert it to an unheated greenhouse. The temperature never drops below the mid-fifties because of the heat radiating through from the house.

"During winter I can grow many plants not naturally adapted to the Valley Forge area—citrus, for instance. When they bloom the fragrance is wonderful.

"With the warm weather of summer, the character of my deck changes completely. We spend much more time outdoors, of course, so the deck becomes as much a social room as a garden. At that time I'll dress it up some with colorful annuals. Yours truly, Kathleen Buchanan"

The judges singled out Kathleen's entry for one very important reason: her deck is truly a garden, not just decoration. It's year round in a climate that precludes winter gardening for many, and it seems to include the best characteristics of a greenhouse and a deck.

Award of Merit, Small-Space Gardening Contest, 1979
Joseph F. Landsberger

"My garden is in my house. It's a back stairway in a large house which has been subdivided into apartments. Since the stairway is blocked off to the second floor and no longer functional, I removed one wall facing my living room (leaving some beams) and paneled the other wall. Two high-intensity and one 'plant' fluorescent bulbs provide the lighting.

"I rotate plants in the room from my collection of over 100. My apartment receives only east light so the room must provide all the rest that plants need. There is also an aquarium to provide humidity.

"To elevate the plants I have added shelving and beneath them there is storage space for my indoor gardening supplies.

"My collection of plants includes a diversity of orchids, bromeliads and succulents as well as many other indoor trees. Sincerely, Joseph Landsberger"

Judge Alan Goldowski: "This idea is more interesting to me in terms of a problem space and a solution to it. Mr. Landsberger converted useless space into a garden."

Judge Mildred Mathias: "It's a clever idea. It could be modified with imagination in any apartment and it gives us an idea of what is possible. I like the use of the aquarium to keep the humidity up. What about a waterfall?"

Above left: Kathleen Buchanan's deck/garden in winter. Note that when the panels are removed the greenhouse-like area is transformed into an open deck. Above: Joseph Landsberger turned the space under an unused staircase into a satisfactory growing environment. See text above.

71

Windowboxes

It's unfortunate that windowboxes are not as popular in America as they are in other countries. They add a quality of their own to houses and other buildings, one that usually leaves a lasting impression on visitors and neighbors alike.

Windowboxes represent a special form of container gardening. The basics are the same when planting in windowboxes as in any other container. But there are special considerations of weight and drainage, as well as the need for securely attaching the box to a ledge or railing.

To begin, you need a suitable box. Nurseries and garden centers abound in ready-made boxes, most of which are perfectly suitable for a variety of uses. Many gardeners, however, prefer to make their own boxes, custom-fitted for a particular place. If you plan to construct your own box, the first choice of wood would be redwood, cedar, cypress or seasoned black locust, all of which naturally resist the damaging effects of moisture. If you choose redwood, it should be heart grade (solid red color, with no lighter streaks of sapwood), and air or kiln dried to prevent later warping or cracking.

Other types of wood to consider are pine and fir,

Simple but effective small windowbox planted with a profusion of geraniums lends a friendly atmosphere to the exterior of this house.

both of which should be treated with a wood preservative containing copper naphthanate or copper sulfate, which are not injurious to plants. Do not use wood preservatives containing pentachlorophenol, which remains toxic to plants for a number of years.

The size of the box is up to you, but a few general guidelines should be considered. The box should be 7 to 10 inches deep and 10 or 11 inches wide. Boxes over 5 feet in length are difficult to handle, especially when filled with soil. The optimum length is approximately 3 feet.

The box should be held together with wood screws rather than nails, which can loosen and dislodge over a period of time. Adequate drainage can be provided with ½-inch holes spaced 5 inches apart. If you plan to fill the box with a lightweight soil mix, cover the holes with a fine mesh screen such as aluminum fly screen. If the box is intended to stand on a flat surface, small pieces of 1-inch wood under each corner will act as "feet" and allow drainage.

Using redwood or cedar to construct the boxes has an advantage in that both woods weather attractively without paint or stain. If you plan to paint your windowbox, favor the light colors—they reflect sunlight and keep the soil within the box from getting too warm and damaging the roots.

Fastening windowboxes to window sills or narrow ledges should be done with the utmost care. Take a careful look at the photos on page 73 for some secure, worry-free methods.

In all cases, the soil for the boxes should be one of the synthetic soil mixes. Garden stores everywhere sell special container mixes under a wide variety of trade names—Redi-Earth, Jiffy Mix, Metro Mix, Super Soil, Pro-Mix and many others. The advantages of these mixes are too numerous to ignore: they're disease-free, provide great drainage and a near perfect medium for root growth, and most importantly, are significantly lighter than the average garden soil.

Plants in windowboxes need the same attentive care that any plant in a container demands. A long weekend of neglect when you're away may be more than a thriving windowbox display can stand. During the warm summer months, daily watering is usually necessary, and frequent, light applications of fertilizer help compensate for the limited root zone.

Plants to go in the boxes can be all of one type or a mixture of forms, varieties and colors. A window box 11 inches wide can handle 3 rows of plants, and we've seen some very attractive combinations of tall upright forms, bushy habits, and trailing varieties. Generally speaking, plants for windowboxes should have a lengthy season of bloom. Try to keep plants under 18 inches in height to prevent wind damage.

The location of the boxes will, to a large degree, determine the selection of the plant material. The following sample lists are arranged by various exposures.

Flowers for windowboxes

In full sun, upright:

Ageratum houstonianum	Ageratum; annual
Calendula officinalis	Calendula; annual
Callistephus chinensis	Asters; annual
Chrysanthemum species	Chrysanthemum; perennial
Dianthus species	Pinks; perennial
Matthiola incana	Stocks; annual
Phlox paniculata	Phlox; perennial
Salvia species	Salvia; annual
Tagetes species	Marigold; annual
Zinnia elegans	Zinnia; annual

In full sun, trailing:

Dimorphotheca sinuata	Cape marigold; annual
Lobelia erinus	Lobelia; annual
Lobularia maritima	Sweet alyssum; annual
Pelargonium peltatum	Geranium; perennial
Sanvitalia procumbens	Sanvitalia; perennial
Thunbergia alata	Black-eyed Susan vine; annual
Tropaeolum majus	Nasturtium; annual
Verbena x hybrida	Verbena; annual
Vinca species	Periwinkle; perennial

In shade or semi-shade, upright:

Begonia cucullata	Begonia, fibrous; annual
Caladium x hortulanum	Caladium; perennial
Calceolaria crenatiflora	Calceolaria; perennial
Cyclamen persicum	Cyclamen; perennial
Fuchsia x hybrida	Fuchsia, upright varieties; perennial
Primula species	Primula; annual
Senecio x hybridus	Cineraria; annual
Torenia fournieri	Torenia; annual

In shade or semi-shade, trailing:

Browallia species	Bush violet; annual
Fuchsia x hybrida	Fuchsia, trailing varieties; perennial
Hedera species	Ivy; perennial
Iberis sempervirens	Candytuft; perennial
Impatiens species	Impatiens; annual
Tropaeolum majus	Nasturtium; annual
Viola species	Viola; annual

Shown above is a construction sequence for window boxes that surround a bay window. Three nursery redwood planters, large enough to hold 6 inch pots, were mounted on brackets and painted. Moss is used to surround pots and cover tops and aid in moisture retention and insulation. Using nursery-bought color, planter can always have a "fresh-planted" look.

Big Harvests

*You can grow fresh, high quality fruits &
vegetables in the smallest of spaces. With
containers and dwarf plant varieties, the
possibilities are endless.*

If you have ever tasted home garden tomatoes, just-picked ears of corn, or fresh strawberries and peaches, then you know the difference between what you can buy at the market and what you can grow. This is no criticism of the markets that supply such a variety and abundance of fresh goods, but a loss of flavor and freshness is part of the price we pay.

Home garden vegetables are picked at full ripeness, not before. They don't have to be tough enough to withstand shipping. The taste difference alone has turned many gourmet cooks into vegetable gardeners as well. Convenience is another factor. It's much simpler and more satisfying to step out to the garden for some sprigs of parsley, a few spinach leaves or green onions than to drive to the store.

But then comes the problem so many of us are faced with: little or no actual garden space. On page 79 there is a plan for a very productive vegetable garden. The plants were all grown in containers and required only 120 square feet. This is an indication of the substantial vegetable production possible in relatively small spaces.

Fruit plants can be a part of the landscape. Strawberries make a good ground cover. Apples are available in varieties and sizes to suit large or small gardens in nearly any climate. Dwarf citrus trees (where climate permits), genetic dwarf peaches and espaliered pears are other possibilities.

Vegetables

The first question is, how small a container is big enough for various vegetables? Container size has little if any bearing on growth, except for the root crops—carrots and beets—which need a slightly deeper container.

The biggest problem with small containers is keeping the plant supplied with water and nutrients. The growth and fruit set of a full-size tomato in a 6-inch pot is amazing, but it will probably need watering at least twice daily. Eventually, the small container gets filled with only roots, leaving little or no room for a moisture reservoir. Therefore, the minimum size container in which a plant can be grown is not always the most practical.

Over the years we have used all sizes of pots, cans, plastic buckets, plastic trash containers, garbage cans, bulb pots, fiber pots, paint buckets, half-barrels and more. They vary considerably in length of useful life, local availability, cost and appearance, but not in how well the plants grow within them.

The advantage of a large container is that the larger volume of soil holds more water and nutrients. Watering and feeding is less a chore than when plants are confined to smaller containers. But on the other hand, it makes no sense to provide a larger container than is necessary. This is especially true when gardening on a balcony or roof where keeping weight to a minimum is important.

When you grow vegetables in containers, you can take advantage of the various microclimates around the house and garden. The heat-loving eggplant can be placed where it receives not only full sunlight but also reflected heat from a south wall.

Maybe you've heard before that vegetable gardens need to be grown in "full sunlight." Many will tolerate filtered shade. Bend the rules to discover what works for your plants.

The following descriptions emphasize dwarf or compact varieties grown in containers. Containers and raised beds are two of the best solutions to the small- or no-space garden problems so common today.

At left, a "garden for all reasons." The maker of this garden has experimented for several seasons with ways to maximize production in his narrow and small space. Just about every plant visible in this picture is growing in a container. Make no mistake, there's plenty of upkeep involved, but the returns are great.

Vegetables

Top three photographs show sweet potato production in a five gallon container. Wilted tops indicate mature crop. Bottom two photographs illustrate possibilities of Irish potato crop grown in a bushel basket. If possible, protect baskets with plastic liner.

Beets

Season: best growth is during the cool weather of spring and fall.
Light: will tolerate some shade.
Spacing: keep them 2 to 3 inches apart.
Container: at least 8 inches deep.
Comments: beets need to be thinned because more than one plant comes from each seed (an exception is 'Mono-King Explorer'). Wait until the tops are about 7 inches high before thinning. Greens can be used in the kitchen like spinach. Sow directly into the container; don't transplant.

Varieties: 'Golden Beet' and 'Detroit Dark Red' are two popular ones. Miniatures that can be grown in an even smaller container include 'Spinel', 'Baby Canning Beet', and 'Best of All'.

Cabbage

Season: takes frost, so set plants out as soon as the soil can be worked in spring. A good winter crop in mild climate areas.
Light: should have full sun.
Spacing: in a box, plant no closer than 12 inches. They're better planted in individual containers.
Container: 5 gallon size or larger.
Comments: requires good care to form solid heads when grown in containers. Even then, most varieties will form somewhat smaller heads. Early (short season) types are generally best.
Varieties: 'Dwarf Morden' matures fast, forming softball-size heads. 'Baby Head' is even smaller but head is very hard.

Cantaloupe

Season: like all the melons and squashes, needs plenty of summer heat. Plant after frost danger, in the warmest corner of the garden.
Light: full sun.
Spacing: plant 18 to 24 inches apart or in individual containers.
Container: plants are better off in a large container—5 gallon or bigger—during summer's heat.
Comments: standard-size cantaloupes (or muskmelons) can be trained along a trellis. Use cheesecloth, strips of worn-out nylons or similar soft material to tie the developing melons to the trellis. Total production from dwarf cantaloupes is usually less than from full-size types.
Varieties: 'Minnesota Midget' is a common small variety with high quality fruits. Others include 'Dwarf' or 'Bush Muskmelon' and 'Short 'n Sweet'.

Carrots

Season: best growth is during the cool weather of spring, early summer and fall.
Light: will tolerate partial shade.
Spacing: thin to 1½ to 3 inches apart.
Container: a box about 10 inches deep is good but if you plant a very short variety, a shallower container will do.
Comments: Don't transplant carrots or they will probably become forked. Make sure the variety you plant isn't longer than the container is deep.
Varieties: 'Nantes Half Long' and 'Royal Chantenay' are the largest size practical for containers. Try some of the midget carrots: 'Tiny Sweet', 'Little Finger', 'Sucram' (most popular baby carrot in Europe and very sweet), 'Baby Finger' (also very sweet), 'Short 'n Sweet', 'Bunny Bite' (among the shortest at 2 inches long), and 'Gold Nugget' (2 to 3 inches long and almost as wide).

Chives

Season: hardy perennial.
Light: best in partial shade.
Spacing: plant clusters 2 to 3 inches apart.
Container: they'll do well in a 4-inch pot.
Comments: start with small plants. They will spread fast. Attractive lavender flowers will appear in summer if leaves are left unclipped.
Varieties: any.

Corn

Season: likes summer heat.
Light: full sun.
Spacing: 10 to 14 inches between plants: 30 to 36 inches between rows in a garden. Overplanting will reduce yields, although some dwarf varieties can be planted more closely.
Container: large containers or planters big enough for several plants are best. A 12-inch pot would be the minimum for a single plant.
Comments: a problem with container corn is poor pollination. Corn is wind pollinated and usually planted in blocks of several rows. Plant in groups to the extent possible.
Varieties: 'Golden Midget' develops 4-inch ears and the whole plant grows to only 3 feet. Similar are: 'Golden Miniature' with 5-inch cobs, 'Midget Hybrid', 'Masons Midget', and 'Fiarbo Golden Midget'.

Clockwise from bottom left: Innovative gardener conducted lettuce-growing experiments in an "ideal" environment. Several varieties were grown individually in one gallon containers. Above, a potpourri of vegetables in containers, including beans on a trellis and a bush type squash. Top right: Inexpensive containers— large size, heavy weight garbage bags produce a bountiful potato crop. Bottom right: Small size greenhouse for vegetable starts vents quickly when roof panels are removed.

Cucumber

Season: needs summer heat.
Light: requires full sun.
Spacing: set plants 12 to 18 inches apart.
Container: can grow successfully in containers as small as 8 inches but larger ones will usually be more practical.
Comments: the strong-growing, standard-size types can be easily trained to a trellis. Cucumbers that form hanging down will grow straight. The more space-saving types are listed below.
Varieties: 'Pot Luck' is one of the best. It forms 6 to 7-inch fruits but the vine is extremely compact. 'Patio Pik' is another very reliable container cucumber. Other space-savers include 'Bush Whopper', 'Cherokee 7' and 'Spacemaster'.

Eggplant

Season: frost sensitive; needs summer heat.
Light: full sun.
Spacing: one plant per container works best.
Container: 4 or 5 gallon size.
Comments: in containers, the varieties with medium to small-size fruits high on the plant are more attractive than the lower-growing, heavy-fruited varieties. Standard varieties require high heat and long growing seasons, so choose early-maturing kinds if you are in a short season area or can't give the plants full sun exposure.
Varieties: 'Dusky' is a medium-size plant but does well in containers. 'Ichiban' is a good container variety with medium-size fruit.

Lettuce

Season: early spring, late summer or fall is best. Most varieties go to seed ("bolt") during long days of summer.
Light: tolerates partial shade.
Spacing: leaf lettuce can be planted close—4 to 5 inches apart. Give head-forming lettuce about 10 inches between plants.
Container: just about any container will do.
Comments: crisphead types are generally less successful in containers. Lettuce grows fast and can be planted every few weeks in a container garden. Avoid extreme watering.
Varieties: 'Tom Thumb' is a bona-fide dwarf lettuce. A butterhead type, it is small enough when mature to be served intact. Many other varieties will do well in containers. Some good ones are: 'Green Ice', 'Oak Leaf', 'Deer's Tongue' and 'Buttercrunch'.

Onions

Season: generally, plant in very early spring and harvest in late fall, but the best season depends on the onion variety and your climate.
Light: partial shade is fine for green onions. Full sun is necessary for bulb production.
Spacing: 2 to 3 inches apart.
Container: any container 6 inches or more deep.
Comments: Leave one green onion every 4 inches to form a bulb. After tops die back, bulbs can be harvested and stored.
Varieties: many good varieties are available but none is specifically for containers.

Many gardeners are faced with the problem of soil so poor or unusable that an entirely new system needs to be devised if there's to be any garden at all. The rock "soil" of the gardener above is an extreme example. Her solution: reinforced plastic garbage bags filled with a quality soil mix.

Squash

Season: summer.
Light: full sun.
Spacing: 2 to 4 feet apart or individually in containers.
Container: large—18 to 24 inches.
Comments: like pumpkins, these are not space savers but the bush types listed below require less space.
Varieties: 'Bush Acorn Table King,' 'Creamy' (a dwarf yellow straight neck with probably the smallest vine of all the squash), 'Scallopini' (a 1977 All-American Selections medal winner and widely available), 'Table Ace' and 'Golden Nugget.'

Tomatoes

Season: summer. Most varieties will set fruit poorly if night temperatures go below 55° or over 75° F (13° and 24° C).
Light: full sun. Plants will grow and fruit in partially shaded locations, but yield will be reduced.
Spacing: depends on the variety and how trained.
Container: full-size varieties should have a 4 to 5-gallon container. Smaller kinds can be grown in smaller containers.
Comments: hundreds of varieties are available. Your nursery and local extension agent will have advice. Also check Ortho's *All About Tomatoes*. Below are some of the best container varieties for you to try.
Varieties: 'Tiny Tim,' a 12-inch plant with cherry-size fruit, fits easily into a 6 or 8 inch pot. 'Salad Top' produces unusually sweet 1-inch fruits on a 30-inch plant. 'Sugar Lump' stays under 1 foot tall and bears 1-inch fruit. 'Pixie Hybrid' bears clusters of 1¾ inch fruits on 18-inch plants. 'Patio Hybrid' grows to 30 inches and bears 2-inch fruits. 'Tumblin' Tom' bears 1½ to 2-inch fruit on a 2-foot plant.

Watermelon

Season: summer.
Light: full sun.
Spacing: usually 2 to 4 feet apart. Miniatures can be planted closer.
Container: large—18 to 24 inches in diameter and a foot deep. Try a bottomless container.
Comments: short season varieties will produce better in containers, but even they will produce slightly smaller fruit. Expect one or two fruits per vine.
Varieties: watermelon has a true bush habit but the following will spread less vigorously than standard varieties: 'Sugar Baby,' 'Yellow Baby,' 'Yellow Doll' and 'Sugar Doll.'

Peas

Season: a cool season plant. Plant early spring to midsummer. In mild climates, plant in fall, winter or very early spring.
Light: full sun. They'll become spindly if shaded.
Spacing: 6 to 8 inches apart.
Container: just about any container is okay. A long, narrow planter with trellis attached works well for tall-growing types.
Comments: known as "English Peas" in the South to differentiate them from cowpeas.
Varieties: low-growing kinds that don't need staking are easiest to handle. 'Little Marvel' and 'Dwarf Gary Sugar' stay under 2 feet tall.

Peppers

Season: summer.
Light: need full sun.
Spacing: normally 14 to 18 inches apart.
Container: one plant per 2 to 4 gallon container works well.
Comments: very interesting plants, valuable as an ornamental as well as a food plant.
Varieties: choose among the many varieties of both hot and sweet peppers.

Potatoes

Season: late spring, early summer.
Light: need full sun.
Spacing: 12 inches apart; rows 2 feet apart in a garden.
Container: plant one seed piece in a single 5-gallon container just above bottom.
Comments: potatoes form on the stems rising from the seed piece. Cover the plant as it grows with a very loose soil mix so potatoes can be "picked" rather than dug.
Varieties: Some of the best are: 'Irish Cobbler,' 'Norgold Russet,' 'Norland,' Red Pontiac,' 'Superior' and 'White Rose.'

Pumpkin

Season: summer.
Light: full sun is best.
Spacing: for small gardens, plant individually in large containers.
Container: a box or tub 18 to 24 inches in diameter.
Comments: pumpkins are among the most extravagant space users but are mentioned here to bring your attention to more compact, bush varieties.
Varieties: 'Cinderella' will produce 10-pound pumpkins in as little as 6 square feet. 'Spirit' makes 12-inch pumpkins and has a relatively compact vine.

Vegetable growing in small space

Consider this:

The containers in this garden would take up less than 75 square feet of patio, deck or balcony space. We positioned the containers on a 6 by 20 foot balcony this way:

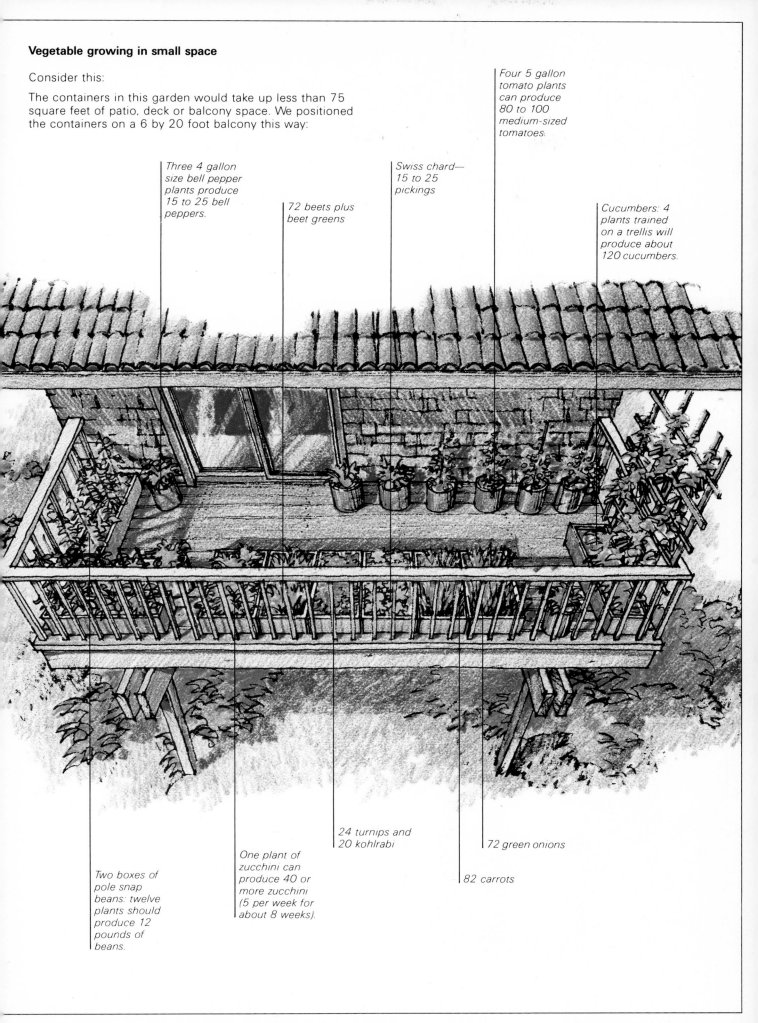

Four 5 gallon tomato plants can produce 80 to 100 medium-sized tomatoes.

Three 4 gallon size bell pepper plants produce 15 to 25 bell peppers.

72 beets plus beet greens

Swiss chard— 15 to 25 pickings

Cucumbers: 4 plants trained on a trellis will produce about 120 cucumbers.

Two boxes of pole snap beans: twelve plants should produce 12 pounds of beans.

One plant of zucchini can produce 40 or more zucchini (5 per week for about 8 weeks).

24 turnips and 20 kohlrabi

82 carrots

72 green onions

Fruits

If you've thought homegrown fruit was too expensive or space consuming, these words from the University of Kentucky Cooperative Extension may change your mind:

"Many fruits can be used as landscape plants and do not need a separate area for proper culture. Also, properly cared for, fruit plantings will pay big dividends in money savings as well as in health and high quality produce, all the time returning great personal satisfaction.

"Tree-ripened fruits in general are much better than commercial, green-picked products. Tree-ripened peaches, for example, gain as much as 300 percent in quality during the last few days of ripening and almost double in volume. Moreover, many of the varieties of fruits grown in commercial orchards do not have the high quality possible in varieties better adapted to home use. This is because the commercial fruits are specially developed to withstand packing and shipping, often at the expense of some quality."

Advantages of dwarf trees. Dwarf varieties of fruit trees have made it possible to grow fruit in confined, urban areas. A genetic dwarf peach, for instance, will fit in the space of a rosebush.

The horticultural work that has produced dwarf fruit trees has been largely supported by commercial growers. For years they have experimented with promising methods of growing fruit crops that can be harvested without having to climb high into the tree with ladders. But non-commercial gardeners are a prime beneficiary of this work. Some advantages of dwarf trees are as follows:

A professional nurseryman experimented to find the maximum number of fruit plants it is possible to grow in a 15 by 50 foot garden.

Dwarf trees bear a crop sooner, often in the second year after planting. Termed "precocious," these early-fruiting trees are a great improvement over a standard tree that needs five to ten seasons to produce its first crop.

Smaller physically, dwarf trees bear less fruit per tree than standard trees. With a few trees of different kinds, you'll have plenty of fruit but not so much at one time that it becomes a problem.

Fruit quality is high. Dwarf trees usually produce larger and more brightly colored fruit than the same variety on a standard tree.

Convenience is a major advantage of dwarf trees. Pruning, spraying and harvesting are all accomplished as you stand on the ground or on a short stepladder.

Dwarf fruit trees do need proper care and won't tolerate neglect. They need about the same level of culture as a modern hybrid tea rose. Watering, for instance, will need to be more frequent than a standard tree requires because the root system of a dwarf tree is more shallow. Also, some kind of artificial support for the tree is usually necessary. This is particularly true of apple trees on Malling 9 and Malling 26 rootstocks.

Berries and currants. Strawberries, blueberries and similar fruits are among the most productive home garden plants. Strawberry plants are probably the easiest to fit into small spaces. As a ground cover, they should be thinned and new plants introduced every three years or so to maintain productivity. Also, planted heavily enough to completely cover the ground, strawberry production will not be at the maximum.

Raspberries and blackberries take up more space but can be grown in large containers. Train them carefully along a fence or trellis and keep them pruned, and they will take up little space but will produce heavy crops of fruit that you just can't buy—the delicate flavors fade during the trip from farm to market.

Blueberries, currants and gooseberries make extremely ornamental shrubs that flower in spring and are covered with fruit in the fall. Blueberries are close relatives of azaleas, so require similar soil: light and slightly acid. The highbush blueberries are most ornamental. Plant two varieties for better crops, about 4 feet apart and at the same level as at the nursery. A heavy mulch is very beneficial.

Both currants and gooseberries are host to a serious disease of five-needle pines, so are prohibited in some areas. Where they can be grown, few plants are as ornamental, easy to grow and productive. Plant them about 4 feet apart and slightly deeper than at the nursery. Use a heavy mulch.

Fruit plants in containers. If you use containers, there's no reason not to try 'Meyer' lemons in Cleveland or peaches in Montana. Tender plants far from their natural climate zone will grow well, provided you move them to shelter when cold weather comes.

However, a fruit tree that is winter-hardy in your area when in the ground may not be hardy in containers. The ground insulates the roots and so keeps them from freezing. Above-ground container soils will freeze more readily. Gardeners in the coldest northern zones should plan to protect even hardy deciduous fruits in the coldest months.

Begin your containerized orchard with containers that are just 2 or 3 inches wider than the root-ball of the plant. If you have a bareroot apple or pear, a 5-gallon container is about right. Evergreen fruits such as citrus should start in a container not much larger than their rootball. Some problems with citrus have been traced to planting too soon in too large a container.

A bushel-basket size of container is about as large as necessary for most fruits. A minimum size is roughly 18 inches square and 18 inches deep. Small containers make more work by increasing the frequency of watering, feeding and root pruning. The right size of container lets the plant find water and nutrients easily, keeps soil from staying too wet around and beneath the roots, and slightly inhibits top growth.

When we discussed container soil mixes (pages 16 to 19) we noted that they should be fast draining. Garden soil alone in a large container usually drains too slowly and may waterlog the roots. Adding amendments such as sand to a mix will make the container heavy and more difficult to move. An artificial soil mix (peat moss plus perlite, for example) has excellent drainage but needs more frequent additions of water and fertilizer. Many gardeners report success with synthetic mix amended by no more than one-third garden loam.

Training fruit plants to fit small spaces
Espaliered fruit trees are usually heavy producers of fruit because the individual branches are fully exposed to the sun. This stimulates heavier flower and fruit production.

Standard trees can be espaliered but dwarfs on a Malling 9 or 27 (the most dwarfing rootstocks), or on Malling 7 or 26, are more commonly used because the growth is less vigorous and therefore there is less need for pruning.

Espaliered apples and pears can be trained against a garage wall or a fence, or along wire supports. In the latter case, the trees themselves will eventually become a fence.

Leave about one foot of space between the wire supports and a wall, especially a hot, west-facing one. Against a garage or house wall, a simple technique is to use strong supports (1-inch galvanized pipe or wood beams) at each corner of the wall or about 8 feet apart. Stretch 12 or 14-gauge wire tightly between the supports using turnbuckles. Each wire will support a horizontal branch. If you are training a standard tree, the first wire should be about 18 inches from the ground; then leave about a foot of space between succeeding wires all the way to the eaves of the building.

Making a living fence of dwarf apples
The simplest kind of espaliered dwarf apple starts like a standard tree, with a couple of supports about 8 feet apart. Stretch wires between them, the first about 2 feet from the ground and the second about 3½ or 4 feet from the ground. Dwarf trees on Malling 9 or 27 should be planted closer—2½ to 3 feet apart. Trees on the larger Malling 7 or 26, or the still larger Merton-Malling 106 should be accordingly farther apart. (Remember, larger trees will permit greater height but will also grow much faster, requiring more frequent pruning.)

Plant bareroot whips—trees 2 or 3 years old with few or no side branches—in front of this wire trellis. The whip should reach above the top of the second wire, but cut it off at planting time to just above the first wire. (Many nurseries will cut back the bareroot trees nearly this far as a common practice.) This pruning will force buds to grow that can be trained to extend along that bottom wire.

In the first season, let the two strongest branches keep growing along the bottom wire. Tie them to the wire loosely with soft garden tape. The top bud is normally dominant and will continue vertical growth at the expense of these side branches. Pinch it back occasionally, slowly allowing it to reach the top wire.

By the third or fourth season, the top bud will have reached the top wire. It is allowed to grow no farther and the two strongest horizontal branches are trained the same as the bottom branches.

Within five to seven years, an 8-foot fence of apple trees trained in this fashion will yield approximately three dozen apples a year, depending on the variety and how well it has grown.

Genetic dwarf apple trees can obviously grow and produce in containers as small as these 12 inch clay pots.

Hedges and arbors

Apples and pears. Both dwarf apples and pears grow and fruit well when trained as hedges on horizontal wires. Use wooden rails instead of wires in very cold climates to avoid the damage that freezing wires may cause. Eventually you will have a hedge about 3 feet wide. If parts of the hedge begin to escape and grow too far outward, trim those branches back to healthy side branches in the spring—May is the best month in most locations. To maintain the proper height of 5 to 8 feet, prune the top growth in May.

Peaches and nectarines. For a hedge, plant as you would a dwarf apple, using 3 wires at 2, 4 and 6 feet. Cut the whips to about 24 inches long and shorten any side branches that point along the fence to 2 buds each. Train all new growth at 45 degrees in both directions.

Fruit will form on the branches that grew the previous summer. For this reason, a peach hedge must have its fruiting wood renewed annually. After leaves have fallen in winter, cut out all branches that have fruited and head back the V-shaped main structure to about the middle wire. During summer, encourage the lower shoots and pinch back the upper growth. Always be sure that new growth is above a bud union.

(Note: In parts of the West, the disease called peach leaf curl will attack peaches and nectarines each year. A fungicide spray containing lime-sulfur, dormant oil or copper is the only way to prevent it.)

Apricots and plums. Use approximately the same techniques described for peaches but instead of annually replacing all the branches that have fruited, remove only about a third after leaf fall; during the summer, pinch back new growth on the remaining branches to 4 or 6 leaves.

Figs. In warm areas where figs grow well, train the young trees to form an irregular, permanent scaffold of trunk plus 2 to 5 short branches. These should be headed at 2 or 3 feet long, with the trunk at 45 degrees. New growth from these scaffolds should be cut to about 15 inches long in winter and thinned so that the summer hedge is contained at the size you wish. These branches may produce a little fruit in the summer. Then, trim them very lightly to hold the hedge shape. The new summer growth will fruit in fall. Figs are likely to sucker badly and will need attention several times during the growing season.

Where figs freeze back occasionally, grow them as shrubs rather than training them as compact trees.

Grapes. In order to prune for maximum production, it is important to know what type of grape you have. Wine grapes and muscadines will usually need spur pruning—cut all side branches of a mature (2-year-old) plant to 2 buds in fall or winter. Mature Thompson seedless and Concord grapes must be cane pruned—do not cut these back to short spurs but instead leave two whole canes from the previous growing season. When fruit forms from side growth along these canes, clip the canes off beyond the next set of leaves.

Either type of grape grows from a permanent trunk or trunk plus arms, and is easily trained to a fence or arbor. Grapes are in fact a favorite arbor vine.

Cane berries. Canes of the previous season can be trained to a fan or column shape against a wall, or used as a fence on a two-wire trellis. New canes should be gathered into loosely tied bundles and pushed lengthwise along the wall or fence until the old canes fruit. After fruiting, cut out the old canes and put the new ones in place. Where disease is a problem, as in many areas of the South, cut and destroy all canes immediately after fruiting and use late summer growth for the following year's crop.

Custom made wooden trellis provides vertical growing space for apples in containers on a balcony garden.

Opposite: Orchard in the air: Several years old, this fruit garden provides a remarkable amount of fruit in this unlikely situation.

Landscaping with fruits

According to the University of Kentucky Cooperative Extension Service, two major trends are reason enough to introduce fruit trees and small fruits to the home landscape. The first of these is our new attitude about landscaping in general. Landscaping of the home grounds long ago progressed beyond mere ornamental decoration to the concept of creating outdoor spaces for living and enjoyment, much like the rooms of a house. Aside from barbecues, there should be elements in these outdoor rooms that maintain interest. Most fruit trees have an extremely showy flowering period, followed by a final gesture of splendid fall color. Enjoyment of the outdoors is certainly heightened by picking a bushel of apples or bringing the pruned branches of a cherry tree indoors for winter forcing.

The second major trend is the rejuvenated interest in food gardening. Improved methods of processing have made more foods more readily available in the markets today than ever before, yet more and more people are planting vegetable gardens. Only a few years ago, the petunia was the number-one seller among bedding plants, but today the tomato has become the plant purchased by more gardeners than any other. We can only guess at the causes of this trend: concern about nutrition; the desire to make more use of the land around our homes; the therapeutic value of producing one's own food. Whatever the reasons, plants that bear fruits, nuts and berries should certainly be included in the home landscape.

Not by bread alone. Commercial practices are naturally directed at maximum yields. The home gardener, however, should be willing to sacrifice some of the harvest for some esthetic effect. A good example is the strawberry as ground cover. Commercial growers plant strawberries in rows spaced with clean, cultivated aisles. Usually the plants themselves are treated as annuals, used only one season. As a home ground cover, strawberries may be allowed to grow very densely for the sake of appearance. Also, a single planting will produce for at least three years. In this situation, production will be lower but the landscape will be more attractive.

Fruit tree forms for landscape use

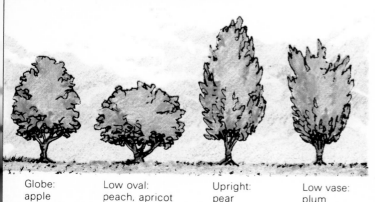

Globe: apple
Low oval: peach, apricot
Upright: pear
Low vase: plum

Include fruits in your plan. The need for a comprehensive landscape plan cannot be overemphasized. When planning your landscape, apply the recommendations of your local agriculture experiment station and nursery, and of publications such as Ortho's *All About Fruits & Berries*.

The first step in evaluating fruit plants for the landscape is to classify them into groups according to their different growth habits. We've talked about espalier training of fruit trees on pages 22 to 23; here we illustrate the different forms of popular fruit plants. Their varied shapes are important to consider before deciding where to locate them in your landscape.

The chart on this page can be an initial guide to the possible landscape use of fruit plants. Mix these plants with ornamentals to obtain the most pleasing effects. But consider the maintenance requirements of each. For example, strawberries may be used as a ground cover under rose bushes, since both will thrive with a winter mulch. However, roses may require spraying just when the berries would be harvested. Since a thorough spraying of the roses may also cause the berries to be drenched with materials not recommended for edible crops, you might want to keep food plants in groups—or mix them with ornamentals that do not require special care.

Fruits for landscaping

Use	Fruit	Spacing
Ground Covers	Strawberry	18-24 in.
Low Shrubs	Gooseberry	3-6 ft
	Currant	3-6 ft
Tall Shrubs	Blueberry	5-8 ft
	Quince	5-8 ft
	Fig	10-12 ft
	Filbert	10-15 ft
	Dwarf citrus	4-10 ft
Climbers	Grape (for arbor)	8-10 ft
	Blackberry (trailing or semi-upright)	8-10 ft
Hedge—Low to Medium	Red, black & purple raspberry	3-4 ft
	Gooseberry	3-4 ft
	Currant	3-4 ft
	Blueberry	3-4 ft
Tall Screen	Dwarf apple	3-6 ft
	Dwarf pear	3-6 ft
	Dwarf peach, plum, nectarine	3-6 ft
Small Trees (Under 20 ft)	Dwarf peach	12-20 ft
	Dwarf apple	12-20 ft
	Dwarf pear	12-20 ft
	Dwarf plum	12-20 ft
	Dwarf cherry	12-20 ft
	Persimmon	12-20 ft
	Quince	12-20 ft
	Apricot	12-20 ft
	Pomegranate	12-20 ft
Large Trees (Over 20 ft)	Apple	20-30 ft
	Pear	20-30 ft
	Cherry	20-30 ft
Suitable for Espaliering	Dwarf Pear	3-6 ft
	Dwarf apple	3-6 ft

Back yard fruit production

Consider these factors:

Many space-saving plants and techniques are available to the backyard fruit grower. Varieties of dwarf and semi-dwarf fruit trees, berries and fruiting vines can be combined for a landscape high in both efficiency and beauty.

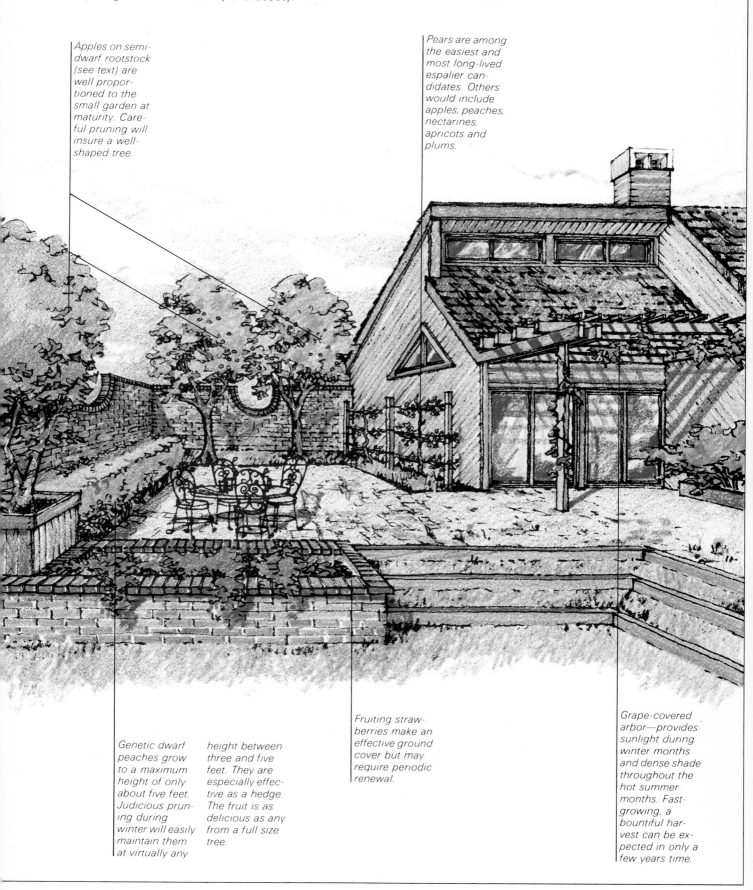

Apples on semi-dwarf rootstock (see text) are well proportioned to the small garden at maturity. Careful pruning will insure a well-shaped tree.

Pears are among the easiest and most long-lived espalier candidates. Others would include apples, peaches, nectarines, apricots and plums.

Genetic dwarf peaches grow to a maximum height of only about five feet. Judicious pruning during winter will easily maintain them at virtually any height between three and five feet. They are especially effective as a hedge. The fruit is as delicious as any from a full size tree.

Fruiting strawberries make an effective ground cover but may require periodic renewal.

Grape-covered arbor—provides sunlight during winter months and dense shade throughout the hot summer months. Fast-growing, a bountiful harvest can be expected in only a few years time.

Community Gardens

A recent poll revealed that nearly 2 million Americans are involved in community gardening. There are good reasons for this activity. Community gardens provide gardening space to those with little or none of their own. Community gardens are educational. And they can have a revitalizing effect on tired neighborhoods.

The economic advantages of community gardening should be obvious to anyone who pays grocery bills. According to the California Council for Community Gardening, the average home or community vegetable plot nationwide in 1977 was 750 square feet, cost about $25 to get going and yielded $375 in savings on food bills. For people who needn't be concerned with the economic advantages, the nutritional and psychological benefits of growing their own vegetables are invaluable.

Community gardens of the modern type are a fairly recent development but the precedent is old. In England they are known as allotment or "guinea" gardens (because the rent was one guinea per year) and can be traced back as far as the 18th century.

Community gardens today take many forms. At one project in Terra Linda, California, the gardener rents a plot of about 15 by 25 feet on the grounds of a local elementary school. The program is coordinated by the city parks and recreation department and the charge is $15 per year. Another in the San Francisco bay area brings teenagers and senior citizens together and is funded by the federal government (Office on Aging, Title VII). The heavy work is done by the teenagers and the harvest is used by the seniors.

Many schools across the country have found educational value in group gardening. School gardens aren't new—the Cleveland Public School District has had a gardening program since the turn of the century—but they are now in a phase of renaissance.

At planting time there's plenty of activity in a community garden as all hands join in. Many local programs are being started in an increasing number of urban areas.

Government participation in community gardening is well established. In 1978, sixteen cities received money from the U.S. Department of Agriculture, helping them to establish and maintain community gardens. The cities: Atlanta, Baltimore, Boston, Cleveland, Jacksonville, Memphis, Milwaukee, Newark, New Orleans, St. Louis, New York, Chicago, Los Angeles, Philadelphia, Detroit and Houston. Today the federal support is diminishing but several states are continuing to support established programs. The nationwide Cooperative Extension Service, with connections to both the U.S. Department of Agriculture and the local land-grant universities, usually coordinates these programs.

How to start a community garden. The Cooperative Extension Service is the best place to start. It will be included with the county listings in your phone book under "Cooperative Extension," "Farm Advisor," or "County Agent." Or write to Gardens for All, whose address is given on page 111.

At least two states offer good organization primers. The New Hampshire Cooperative Extension provides the pamphlet, *Organizing Neighborhood Gardens for Your Community;* and the California Service offers *Community Gardening in California.*

New garden pitfalls. If you are aware of possible problems at the outset, much can be done to avoid them. To survive, a community garden must overcome many obstacles, including the quality of the soil and the organization of the gardeners.

Soil in urban areas is commonly poor. In many cases topsoil was removed years before. Put soil-building high on your priorities because the plants will then grow better and so will the gardeners' enthusiasm. Let Cooperative Extension agents help. They frequently know of abundant sources of manures, tree chippings or other inexpensive organic matter. They will save you a great deal of time and money.

Consider installing permanent raised beds. One community garden used 12-inch-high raised beds filled with good soil mix. Pathways between the beds were mulched heavily with tree chips. The first year the plants grew beautifully, and the weed problem that can so completely discourage new gardeners was avoided.

New gardens may have problems supplying an adequate quantity of water to all the participants. Good vegetables need plenty of water. Getting enough water to your garden is another way that Cooperative Extension expertise can be a great help.

Finally, good organization is important. Don't be too casual, especially at first. New gardens need at least one person willing to be responsible for necessary coordinating of work days and contacting outside help when necessary.

Distant highrises provide a dramatic backdrop to the simple beauty of this community garden/park.

Notebook

*The best ideas and recommendations
for the ideal trees, shrubs, ground covers,
vines, perennials, and annuals for
small gardens.*

The purpose in these following pages is simple: to introduce you to some of the finest plants for small gardens. Without any doubt, our recommendations are arbitrary. Many more plants than we could possibly mention are or could be suitable for small space gardens. But our suggestions are based both on the personal experience of several of our editors and the experience of nurserymen and plantsmen throughout the country. In this way the following plants serve as a basic guide to small space landscaping. Combine our recommendations with those of your nurseryman to make the best possible choices.

Trees for small gardens are discussed on pages 90 to 95. One of the most important and often toughest choices to make, we devote the most space to them. There are general suggestions as well as comments about trees for both mild and cold climates. For important information on topics such as growth rates, hardiness, and specific cultural requirements, refer to a good plant encyclopedia such as Ortho's *The World of Trees.* Also, don't neglect your nurseryman as a source of good information about local growing conditions.

Shrubs are usually not as visually dominant so don't attract the attention of trees, but in a small garden are often just as important. The specific distinction between "trees" and "shrubs" is always hard to make. In many of the gardens pictured throughout this book, shrubs have been allowed to reach their full height and lower branches removed making them in most important ways, trees. Check the list "Shrubs that can be trained into trees" on page 95.

Ground covers, beginning on page 98, are the unifiers of the landscape. They tie together the desparate elements of garden paving, shrubs and trees. As they fill in, the necessary "finished" look evolves. Many varieties of plants can work as ground covers. Choose a height, texture and growth habit that suits your need.

Vines are a charming and satisfying addition to most every garden. Beginning on page 101, we describe several of the best and list vines for special situations. Vines blend together vertical elements of the garden. They can cover architectural mistakes or similar unattractive views. Look especially to the fast growing annual vines. Many unusual ones are listed (available from local sources or one of the seed companies listed under "Sources") that will add considerable interest and fun to a summer garden.

The perennials, pages 103 to 104, are usually the landscape standouts. The word brings first to the mind of many thoughts of the classical English border full of rare or otherwise hard-to-grow special plants. But in fact, perennials are as variable as any other grouping of plants and can be used in many ways. Some are commonly grouped and allowed to form a permanent ground cover. Others are planted singly to provide an accent or focal point. Whatever your need, we urge you to consider them.

Annuals are the flashy, summertime performers. Most common perhaps are the colorful marigolds and petunias which no summer garden should be without. However you may desire to use them—as a dominant theme or for spots of color—read some of our comments beginning on page 105. They're the result of several years test garden experience.

Whether you read these pages straight through or simply use the lists for a quick reference, we think you'll become much better acquainted with the choice plants for small gardens.

Few plants brighten a shade garden as well as tuberous begonias. Mixed with the begonias are a few flowers of impatiens.

Trees

To many people, there seems to be an obvious contradiction to any conversation that includes trees and small-space gardening. Just the word "trees" conjures up thoughts of massive maples and pines or stately oaks. How could anything so large be considered where space is the limiting factor?

Actually, trees play a very important role in the small garden. Apart from such characteristics as spectacular flowers and fall color, cultivars (cultivated varieties) have been developed with predictable, distinctive forms. From columnar to pyramidal to spreading, there is a tree just right for every spot. Additionally, many of the giants can be brought down to size by restricting their root space in containers, and as many expert small-space gardeners already know, trees are one of the best uses of vertical space where there is little horizontal space.

In minimum-space gardening, selecting the right tree for your garden is very important. In close quarters, you'll be living right with these trees. Their virtues and vices will be accentuated. Besides the obvious qualities of a tree—flowers, fall color, pleasant foliage and its form—don't forget attractive bark or interesting branching patterns. They can give a dramatic presence.

You can also think of trees as problem-solvers, blocking unsightly views or wind, or providing cooling shade. Select a tree for more than one good quality; it will give you the longest season of pleasure.

Consider, too, whether you want a deciduous or evergreen tree, its rate of growth and, of course, its hardiness. Refer to the section on fruit trees, pages 80 to 85; many make fine small-garden and patio trees.

Japanese flowering cherry
(Prunus serrulata)

Pruning shears are an all-important companion for the small space gardener. Never be afraid to bring them out and use them vigorously whenever a plant reaches beyond its limits.

It's a pleasant surprise to many first-time pruners to see that pruning can so dramatically enhance a plant's appearance. Removal of smaller or lower limbs tends to accentuate branching patterns. Trees that periodically reach too high for a given area can be easily kept down to size. Proper pruning requires only a little knowledge of how plants grow, and some experience. Refer to Ortho's *All About Pruning* for more details.

Maples. As a beautiful foliaged deciduous tree, the Japanese maple (*Acer palmatum*) commands respect. Many varieties, with a wide range of leaf forms, leaf colors (mostly shades of green, red or purple) and intriguing branching patterns, are available. The leaves range from the common 5-lobed maple type to the 'Dissectum' with finely divided feathery leaves. Most have brilliant fall color and are ideal for containers. They rarely exceed 15 to 25 feet and can be grown in sun or shade.

Other small maples worth considering include the hedge maple (*Acer campestre*), the trident maple (*Acer buergeranum*), and the amur maple (*Acer ginnala*).

Some of the larger maples are also available in very useful, smaller cultivars. Others have unique forms that are ideal for those difficult small-space situations. For example, the species Norway maple (*Acer platanoides*) typically grows upwards of 70 feet. There are over 20 varieties available in almost every shape, size and foliage color. 'Almira' is a small version, rarely exceeding 25 feet. 'Erectum' is a very narrow-growing cultivar useful in corners or against walls.

Redbuds. The Eastern redbud (*Cercis canadensis*) is an excellent four-season performer ideal for small spaces. It has beautiful pink to red, pear shaped flowers in spring; pleasant green, heart shaped leaves in summer; yellow fall color; and interesting pods and reddish bronze bark on horizontally tiered branches in winter. It grows fast into a 25 to 35 foot irregular round headed tree. 'Alba' has white flowers. 'Forest Pansy' has purple foliage and red bark.

Pears. There are several members of the pear family (*Pyrus* species) that are well adapted to small spaces. The first is the callery pear (*Pyrus calleryana*) and its cultivars. They are tough, deciduous trees with bright white flowers in spring. Leaves are shiny green, becoming brilliant in fall. The varieties 'Bradford,' 'Chanticleer,' and 'Aristocrat' are thornless. A common street tree, the callery pear can be large at maturity (40 to 50 feet), but the variety 'Faureri' rarely grows taller than 20 feet and is appreciated for its prolific flowering.

Another good pear, the evergreen pear (*Pyrus kawa-*

kami), is described as a part of the section on trees for mild climates.

Redbud *(Cercis canadensis)*

Dogwood *(Cornus florida)*

English holly *(Ilex aquifolium)*

Silverbells. A popular native of the eastern states, this tree *(Halesia carolina)* deserves much more use in small gardens. In mid-spring, each twig bears a string of one-inch long white flowers like little wedding bells. It grows slowly to 25 or 30 feet and is usually multistemmed. Another important attribute for small gardens is the dark and uniquely scaled bark.

A close relative, the mountain silverbell *(Halesia monticola)* is also useful in small gardens, in patios or near entryways.

Either tree normally casts light shade that is ideal for growing such plants as rhododendrons and azaleas beneath them.

Hawthorns. The hawthorns are another large family of valuable small trees. Beautiful foliage, profuse late spring flowers, bright red berries, and splendid fall color are their virtues. The Washington thorn *(Crataegus phaenopyrum)* has the best fall color of the hawthorns. Its shiny green leaves turn bright orange red in fall.

In areas without much summer heat and humidity, try the English hawthorn *(Crataegus laevigata)*. It comes in a variety of flower forms and colors (white, pink and red). Popular cultivars include 'Alba Plena' and 'Autumn Glory' with white flowers. 'Paulii' and 'Crimson Cloud' have flowers in shades of red and pink.

Other good hawthorns include the very hardy, white flowered Crataegus 'Toba,' *Crataegus vancrudis*, 'Winter King' with glossy foliage and long-lasting berries; and the large, white flowered Lavelle hawthorn *(Crataegus lavelli)*. Most hawthorns are round-headed trees averaging about 15 to 25 feet.

Magnolias. No conversation on small-space trees would be complete without considering the magnolias. Even the grand old Southern magnolia *(Magnolia grandiflora)* which can reach 80 feet is available in cultivars, like 'St. Mary,' that rarely exceed 20 feet. For spectacular deciduous magnolias, consider the saucer magnolia *(M. soulangiana)* and the Merrill magnolia *(M. loebneri* 'Merrill'), among others. All provide huge flowers (some before the leaves unfold) with artistic branching and dramatic foliage.

Fringe tree. With a little help from pruning shears, the fringe tree *(Chionanthus virginicus)* makes a showy patio tree. It grows slowly to between 20 and 30 feet, and has a narrow oblong crown. An attractive multi-trunked tree, it has fleecy clusters of white spring flowers. The bold, heavy textured foliage turns yellow before dropping in fall.

Dogwoods. In areas with slightly acid soils, the dogwoods are prime candidates for small-space gardens. The flowering dogwood *(Cornus florida)* is by far the most popular member of this large family of trees and shrubs. A native of the eastern United States, it rarely exceeds 25 to 30 feet in height. It provides year-round beauty, starting with the wonderful white or pink flowers in spring. In fall, the leaves turn rich red and crimson, followed in winter by glossy red fruits on the horizontally layered branches. Some of the best cultivars include 'Cherokee Chief' with deep red flowers, and 'Cloud Nine' and 'Fragrant Cloud' with white flowers.

Other dogwoods to consider include the Chinese dogwood (*Cornus kousa*), and the yellow-flowering Cornelian cherry (*Cornus mas*) with bright red edible fruit. In the northwest, don't forget the mountain dogwood (*Cornus nutallii*).

Needled evergreens. There is an endless list of needled evergreens that can fit into the small garden. Nurseries making selections have concentrated on bringing these giants down to size as well as choosing new foliage colors. Other species are naturally small, and many of the giants can be miniaturized in containers.

The mountain pine (*Pinus mugo*) is a popular needled evergreen. It spreads low and rarely exceeds 4 feet. Other widely used conifers that have miniature cultivars include the balsam fir (*Abies balsamea*), the false cypress (*Chamaecyparis* species)—of which the dwarf Hinoki (*C. obtusa*) is one of the best—dwarf Japanese cedars (*Cryptomeria*

Above: Flowering plum (*Prunus cerasifera* 'Thundercloud')
Left: Japanese flowering cherry (*Prunus serrulata*)

japonica), several junipers, the spruces (*Picea* species), the arborvitae (*Thuja* species), and the hemlocks (*Tsuga* species). These among many others can have dramatic combined or singular effects, and can be artistically pruned or grown in containers.

For mild climates

For gardeners in mild regions of the South and especially the West who want an evergreen tree, the eucalyptus family offers a wide range of beautiful forms. All are fast growers. One of the good smaller eucalyptus is the *E. cineria* with interesting blue-gray foliage and rough brown bark. It eventually reaches 30 to 40 feet. For bright red flowers, choose the heavy foliaged *E. ficifolia* which stays down to 25 feet with equal spread. *E. pulchella*, one of the peppermint gums, has long narrow leaves and a weeping habit; it grows to between 25 and 30 feet. Three other good flowering eucalyptus are *E. caesia*, *E. erythrocorys* and *E. torquata*. Don't be afraid to try some of the larger eucalyptus in containers.

Where temperatures never drop below freezing choose between one of the many ornamental figs. Indian laurel, *Ficus microcarpa nitida*, makes an ideal evergreen tub and stands well to city conditions.

There are several varieties of *Podocarpus* that will bring a unique texture into any garden. They can reach full size—60 to 70 feet—in their native habitat, but are normally kept much lower by either growing in containers or periodic pruning. They are tender plants but are adaptable to indoor conditions as well as outdoors.

Graceful is the word that best describes the foliage of *Podocarpus*. Long, narrow bright green leaves on drooping branches create a fern-like appearance. Versatile, they adapt well to oriental-style gardens, trimmed to a neat hedge or trained as an espalier.

The two most used species are the yew pine (*Podocarpus macrophyllus*) and the soft textured fern pine (*Podocarpus gracilor*). *Podocarpus macrophyllus maki* is a slower-growing, smaller variety of the yew pine. It reaches only 6 to 8 feet.

The glossy privet (*Ligustrum lucidum*) is another good choice. It stays a very manageable size and is evergreen. It forms a dense crown of glossy green foliage that is especially adaptive to shearing. A close relative is the Japanese privet (*Ligustrum japonicum*). It generally grows lower and has a slightly glossier leaf.

Both privets can take temperatures into the low teens and are especially valuable in areas where there is limited root space.

If these suggestions have not brought you to a decision on the right tree for your garden, look a little further. The sweet bay (*Laurus nobilis*) is a very attractive and well-behaved tree. Its leaves are the bay leaves used as a spice.

Look, too, for the evergreen members of the *Prunus* family. Both the cherry laurel (*Prunus caroliniana*) and Portugal laurel (*Prunus lusitanica*) take well to pruning or shearing, making a good hedge or screen; or they can be left to their natural habits. They'll grow maybe 30 feet high. Both, unfortunately, drop messy fruits.

Even the tenacious olive (*Olea europaea*) has a place in some small gardens. If dropping fruits will make a problem, look for the virtually fruitless variety, 'Swan Hill.'

The evergreen pear (*Pyrus kawakami*) is a well-known small tree. It has beautiful, lustrous green leaves with waved edges and white spring flowers. Besides being an excellent free-standing patio tree, it can easily be espaliered. Rarely does it grow past a 30-foot height.

Full moon maple
(*Acer japonicum*)

Among the good tender evergreen trees for mild areas of the western United States is the strawberry tree (*Arbutus unedo*), with colorful berries and bark. The African sumac (*Rhus lancea*) and *Tristania laurina* also have interesting bark and beautiful foliage. The graceful, weeping habit of the mayten (*Maytenus boaria*) is hard to match. The Australian willow (*Grejera parviflora*) looks like the weeping willow but is smaller. In the mild regions of the Southwest, look for reliable summer bloomers such as the jacaranda (*Jacaranda acutifolia*) or the rosewood tree (*Tipuana tipu*).

For colder climates

In colder climates, look to the hollies among hardy broadleaf evergreen trees. The Wilson holly (*Ilex* 'Wilsonii') forms a small, round headed tree about 15 to 20 feet high. It also makes a fine espalier. The yaupon holly (*Ilex vomitoria*) grows to similar proportions. Both have the typical holly shiny foliage and bright red berries.

Several of the small shrub-type hollies can also be trained as trees.

Many trees can provide spring flower color, but the number of flowering trees decreases as the heat of summer moves in. There are, however, several excellent candidates for the small-space garden. The white, red or lavender-flowering crape myrtle (*Lagerstroemia indica*) is one of the best. It also has good fall color and beautifully peeling, reddish brown bark on muscular branches. It slowly makes a 15 to 25 foot, vase-shaped tree that is especially attractive if multi-trunked.

The golden-rain tree (*Koelreuteria paniculata*) forms a round-headed tree about 20 to 25 feet in height. The yellow summer foliage is followed by interesting seed pods shaped like Japanese lanterns. Three fine summer flowering trees that are unfortunately too often overlooked are the sourwood (*Oxydendrum arboreum*), Korean stewartia (*Stewartia koreana*) and the Japanese snowbell (*Styrax japonicus*). All are extraordinary bloomers and considered by many tree experts to be among the finest trees for American small gardens.

Two large groups of what are normally considered fruiting trees also fit nicely into the small-space scheme. They are the flowering crabapple (*Malus* small fruited species) and the flowering fruits (*Prunus* species) such as plums, cherries and peaches. Besides fragrant spring flowers, both come in myriad shapes, flower and foliage colors, and with or without edible fruit. The flowering fruits include evergreen forms as well as the well-known purple-leaf plums.

When choosing a crabapple, disease resistance is of critical importance. Dr. Lester Nichols of the University of Pennsylvania has been recording susceptibility of the many crabapple varieties to scale, cedar apple rust, mildew and fire blight. Often the most disease resistant varieties are not always the most available. Popular varieties noteworthy for their absence of disease include 'Almey,' 'Flame,' 'Eley,' and 'Hopa.'

The flowering fruits (*Prunus* species) are familiar to even the most casual observer. They include the famous Washington D.C. flowering cherries (*Prunus serrulata* and *P. x yedoensis*), the purpleleaf plums such as *Prunus blireiana* and many other fruiting and non-fruiting flowering trees.

Trees with color in more than one season

These trees provide interest and enjoyment over a long period of time through various combinations of flowers, fruit, autumn color, or interesting bark.

Botanical name	Common name
Amelanchier species	Serviceberry
Cercis canadensis	Eastern redbud
Cornus species	Dogwood
Crataegus species	Hawthorn
Koelreuteria paniculata	Golden-rain tree, varnish tree
Malus species	Crabapple
Oxydendrum arboreum	Sourwood
Prunus species	Flowering fruits
Styrax japonicus	Japanese snowbell

White popular *(Populus alba)*

Trees that can stand abuse

These are the trees to try in that tough spot where too much wind, poor soil, or other difficulties make growing anything a challenge. Some get rather large and may need to be dwarfed by containers.

Botanical name	Common name
Acacia species	Acacia
Acer campestre	Hedge maple
Elaeagnus angustifolia	Russian olive
Eucalyptus species	Eucalyptus
Fraxinus species	Ash
Malus species	Crabapple
Morus alba	Mulberry
Pinus species	Pines
Rhus lancea	African sumac

Trees that are fragrant

Even though some of these trees have flowers that are inconspicuous, their presence in the garden is a pleasure. This list does not include trees whose crushed leaves are fragrant.

Botanical name	Common name
Acer ginnala	Amur maple
Chionanthus virginicus	Fringe tree
Citrus species	Citrus
Hymenosporum flavum	Sweetshade
Magnolia species	Magnolia
Malus species	Crabapples
Osmanthus fragrans	Yellow sweet osmanthus
Oxydendrum arboreum	Sourwood
Prunus species	Flowering fruits

Dogwood *(Cornus florida)*

Shrubs that can be trained into trees

These plants are commonly thought of as shrubs, but by suppressing branches you don't want and encouraging growth upward, they will develop into small trees.

Botanical name	Common name
Hybiscus syriacus	Rose-of-Sharon
Hydrangea species	Hydrangea
Ilex species	Shrub hollies
Nerium oleander	Oleander
Osmanthus species	Osmanthus
Photinia serrulata	Chinese photinia
Prunus species	Flowering fruit trees
Syringa amurensis japonica	Japanese tree lilac
Viburnum species	Viburnum
Wisteria species	Wisteria
Xylosma congestum	Shiny xylosma

Trees that can be miniaturized

Many trees and shrubs can be miniaturized in bonsai style. We can dwarf these naturally by restricting their roots to a small container.

Botanical name	Common name
Acer species	Maple
Cedrus species	Cedar
Cercidiphyllum japonicum	Katsura tree
Chamaecyparis species	False cypress
Cotinus coggygria	Smoke tree
Fagus species	Beech
Ginkgo biloba	Maidenhair tree
Laurus nobilis	Grecian laurel, Sweet bay
Malus species	Crabapple
Pinus species	Pines
Zelkova serrata	Saw-leaf zelkova

Trees that can be sheared

Few trees escape the pruning shears of the home gardener. However, pruning and shearing are good ways of "adapting" large trees to small spaces.

Botanical name	Common name
Cedrus species	Cedar
Cupressocyparis leylandii	Leyland cypress
Cupressus species	Cypress
Ginkgo biloba	Maidenhair tree
Ilex species	Holly
Laurus nobilis	Grecian laurel, Sweet bay
Ligustrum species	Privet
Platanus acerifolia	London plane tree
Platycladus orientalis	Oriental arborvitae
Podocarpus species	Yew pine
Thuja species	Arborvitae

Shrubs

Shrubs are naturals for the small-space garden. Many of them characteristically remain small without a lot of pruning.

The smart small-space gardener uses shrubs like tools, deciding exactly what is needed before buying. You can use shrubs to create lines or soften them. Mass one kind together or line them up to add texture. Use shrubs to blend with or to highlight other garden features and plants. When a spectacular flowering shrub comes into bloom, bring it to center stage in a container.

Shrubs are either deciduous or evergreen, but texture and color of foliage, flowers or fruit are often more important considerations. It is a good idea to see the shrub you plan to buy in a landscape situation before you purchase. The effect it has in a landscape context may be quite different from its appearance in a container by itself.

Shrubs for flowers. A good place to start in any discussions of shrubs is with the most spectacular flowers. Azaleas and rhododendrons appear near the top of the list. Although related, these plants have differences in their basic requirements. But with so many wonderful species and varieties, there is certainly one to fit your climate and color preferences. Some are evergreen, some deciduous, and many have attractive foliage besides beautiful flowers.

The *flowering quince* (*Chaenomeles* species) is one of the first shrubs to bloom in spring. It flowers in a wide range of colors on bare branches that weave an attractive pattern. The shiny green foliage has a red tinge in spring.

Forsythia is another early deciduous bloomer. It bears an abundance of yellow flowers on bare branches. There are several species and varieties to accommodate a variety of positions in the garden.

Where climate permits, evergreen *Camellia* species are an excellent choice for a combination of colorful flowers and shiny foliage.

For fragrance, it is hard to imagine anything sweeter than *Daphne*. Again, there are many varieties but you'll probably be restricted to what is locally available. Still, the fragrant rewards and the attractive foliage make them all worthwhile.

Soft green foliage and large pink, white or blue flowers make the *Hydrangea* a very beautiful shrub. Among the deciduous species, hortensia (*H. macrophylla*) is one of the most popular. All thrive in shade and flower in summer and fall.

The viburnums combine pink to white spring flowers, attractive foliage and colorful berries favored by birds, to become one of the most versatile shrubs. They are available as deciduous or evergreen plants in a variety of forms, many with good fall color.

Other fragrant shrubs with fragrant flowers include the *Gardenia, Jasminum, Osmanthus,* and *Syringa* (lilacs) species. Finally, no small space gardener should do any planting without considering the versatile rose.

Shrubs for foliage. Flower gardens look their best with contrasting foliage. Because of this, or for reasons of texture, you may want a shrub whose main attraction is its foliage. There are many choices: *The barberries* (*Berberris* species) are valuable evergreen and deciduous shrubs, with red foliage and admirable tenacity.

The *Cotoneaster* and *Euonymus* are also good selections. Cotoneaster species range from shrubs to ground covers, with many fine forms from weeping to erect. They have red berries in fall and winter; many deciduous types have good fall color.

Shrub: Burford holly (*Ilex cornuta* 'Burfordii'). Edging: Mondo grass (*Ophiopogon japonicus*).

Spindle trees, especially the evergreen *Euonymus fortunei*, are also valued for their foliage and there are many forms with interesting foliage colors and differing habits.

While considering valuable foliage shrubs, don't forget some of the needled evergreens mentioned as trees (pages 92 to 93). A small tree to one gardener is a shrub to another.

For rich red coloration of spring foliage, consider the *Photinia* and lily-of-the-valley bush (*Peiris japonica*).

Most photinias are evergreen and not extremely hardy. They have clusters of white spring flowers (some fragrant), lustrous red new growth and colorful fruits. Photinias take well to pruning and make an excellent hedge.

The evergreen lily-of-the-valley bush has fiery red foliage in spring, combined with clusters of white flowers. The summer foliage is glossy dark green. Variegated varieties are available.

Other good evergreen foliage shrubs include *Pittosporum*, *Abelia*, the boxwoods (*Buxus* species), and the shiny *Xylosma*. In colder regions, consider the many forms of hollies (*Ilex* species), junipers (*Juniperus* species) and other needled evergreens.

Basic landscape shrubs

Based on both our own experience and surveys of nursery and landscape professionals across the country, here are favorite shrubs for a wide range of climates.

Botanical name	Common name
Abelia 'Edward Goucher'	Goucher abelia
Berberis thunbergii 'Atropurpurea'	Red barbery
Buxus sempervirens	English boxwood
Camellia japonica	Japanese camellia
Camellia sasanqua	Sasanqua camellia
Chaenomeles japonica	Japanese flowering quince
Cotoneaster adpressus praecox	Early cotoneaster
Escallonia bifida	White escallonia
Euonymus fortunei	Winter creeper euonymus
Forsythia x *intermedia*	Border forsythia
Hydrangea quercifolia	Oakleaf hydrangea
Ilex cornuta 'D'Or'	D'Or holly
Ilex crenata	Japanese holly
Juniperus species	Junipers
Ligustrum ovalifolium	California privet
Mahonia aquifolium	Oregon grape
Photinia x *fraseri*	Fraser photinia
Pieris 'Forest Flame'	Forest flame pieris
Pittosporum undulatum	Victorian box
Podocarpus macrophyllus	Yew pine
Pyracantha coccinea	Firethorn
Rhaphiolepis indica	Indian hawthorn
Rhododendron species	Rhododendrons and azaleas
Rosa species	Roses
Syringa vulgaris hybrids	Lilacs
Taxus species	Yews
Viburnum species	Viburnums
Xylosma congestum	Shiny xylosma

Spectacular flowering shrubs

Spring, summer or fall, these are among the best flowering shrubs.

Botanical name	Common name
Azalea species	Azaleas
Buddleia species	Butterfly bush
Camellia japonica	Common camellia
Chaenomeles species	Flowering quince
Cornus mas	Cornelian cherry
Daphne species	Daphne
Forsythia species	Forsythia
Hamamelis species	Witch hazel
Hydrangea species	Hydrangea
Nerium oleander	Oleander
Rosa species	Rose
Spiraea species	Spiraea
Syringa species	Lilac
Viburnum species	Viburnum
Weigela species	Weigela

Shrubs for containers

Most shrubs can be grown in containers. These are some of the finest.

Botanical name	Common name
Azalea species	Azalea
Buxus species	Boxwood
Euonymus europaea	Spindle tree
Ilex species	Holly
Juniperus species	Juniper
Lagerstroemia indica	Crape myrtle
Magnolia species	Magnolia
Nandina domestica	Nandina, Heavenly bamboo
Osmanthus fragrans	Sweet olive, Tea olive
Photinia species	Photinia
Pieris japonica	Lily-of-the-valley bush
Pinus mugo	Mugo pine, Mountain pine
Podocarpus species	Podocarpus
Xylosma congestum	Xylosma

Sasanqua camellia *(Camellia sasanqua)*

Ground covers

To most people, ground covers are low maintenance problem-solvers. Problem-solvers? Without a doubt. But low maintenance? That statement needs to be qualified.

Many ground covers are low maintenance once they are established, but until then, they will need regular water and fertilizer like any other plant. Weeds will have to be dealt with and, before ground covers can be planted, the soil should be thoroughly prepared. Even after they are established, many will need special care to keep them looking their best, which is very important in the small-space garden.

But ground covers can definitely solve many problems. Besides filling spots on slopes or areas under trees, many have beautiful foliage which can create unique textures and exciting contrasts. Others have spectacular flowers.

Choose your ground cover carefully. Ask yourself such questions as, "How will it blend with other plants?" "Will it grow in sun or shade?" And very important to the small space gardener: "Is it too vigorous for my area?" Many ground covers—English ivy and *Hypericum*, for example—can overrun a small garden in a very short time.

Other things to consider include the eventual height off the ground cover. How fast it covers an area will usually determine how many plants you need to buy.

Before selecting one of the plants normally considered as a ground cover, you may want to look at some unlikely candidates. Some annuals make good temporary ground covers: sweet alyssum, verbena, dianthus and creeping zinnia, to name a few. The same is true of many perennials. Some ferns, day lilies, and phlox are good ground covers. Even vegetables such as pumpkins or squash, or fruit plants such as strawberries can be used to cover the ground.

Which ground cover? For a tight, ground-hugging cover, take a look at carpet bugleweed (*Ajuga reptans*). It is a fast-growing, versatile ground cover hardy to -10° F, and adapts to either sun or shade. Bugleweed's main attraction is its handsome, rosette-type foliage. Varieties are available in a range of colors including dark shiny green, bronze, pink and red. As an added bonus, it bears blue spring flowers. Bugleweed is an excellent choice for under trees or along walkways.

If you are looking for a ground cover to grow between stepping stones, something that stays low and can take a little traffic walking over it, there are several alternatives to bugleweed.

Chamomile (*Chamaemelum nobile*) is a favorite choice among tea lovers. Although it will need some shearing to keep it at its lowest, it forms a perfect mat of soft green ferny foliage. It is hardy to 0° F and bears greenish yellow

Above: Wild strawberry *(Fragaria chiloensis)* Right: Mondo grass *(Ophiopogon japonicus)* with clump of *Caladium*.

flowers in summer. When walked on, the leaves add a pleasant fragrance to the air.

Also consider *Sagina subulata*, sometimes called Irish or Scotch moss, for between stepping stones. Differing only in color (Irish is dark green, Scotch light green), they can take temperatures to -30° F, and grow in sun or light shade. The soft texture they yield is hard to match and is particularly appreciated in oriental gardens.

Other ground covers for between-the-steps include lippia (*Phyla nodiflora*), cinquefoil (*Potentilla* species) and thyme (*Thymus* species). They are also valuable for filling nooks and crannies or anywhere the lowest-growing ground cover is desired.

For a completely different texture, try one of the grass-like ground covers. Mondo grass *(Ophiopogon japonicus)*, big blue liriope *(Liriope muscari)* and blue fescue *(Festuca glauca)* are three prime choices.

Mondo grass and liriope are often confused. Both are members of the lily family but liriope has the most spectacular flowers and is hardier (-20° F). It bears violet flower spikes in midsummer. Both mondo grass and liriope are available in a variety of heights and foliage colors.

Blue fescue is an attractive ornamental grass composed of hairlike leaves 4 to 10 inches high in bluish gray tufts. It is very hardy—to -40° F— and makes an excellent accent plant.

Many of the ground covers commonly used in larger areas can also be used tastefully in small spaces. Although they may be more shrubby than such plants as Irish moss or chamomile, they add new dimensions because they have the ability to drape over walls, ledges, or edges of containers.

The low-growing junipers fit into this category. They are very hardy evergreens and are available in many forms and foliage colors. Some of the best include *Juniperus procumbens* 'Nana,' *J. horizontalis* 'Emerald Spreader' or 'Wiltonii,' and *J. sabina* 'Buffalo.' The junipers are excellent utility plants and are valuable used one at a time or in groups.

Various species and varieties of cotoneasters and euonymus are also appropriate ground covers. Most cotoneasters are deciduous and very hardy. Three to look for are the deciduous creeping cotoneaster (*C. adpressus*), cranberry cotoneaster (*C. apiculatus*) and the evergreen *C. dammeri*. There are others, but beware. Cotoneasters spread rather wide, some as much as 10 feet.

The winter creeper (*Euonymus fortunei*) is a hardy evergreen plant that will vine up a wall as well as cover the ground. The best varieties include the purpleleaf winter creeper (*E.f.* 'Colorata'), kew (*E.f.* 'Kewensis'), and the variegated winter creeper (*E.f.* 'Gracilis'). All form low mats rarely exceeding 6 to 10 inches high.

Plants with similar habits and the ability to drape include the red foliaged barberries (*Berberis thunbergii* 'Crimson Pygmy') and the beautifully blue-flowered rosemary (*Rosmarinus officinales* 'Prostratus'). In the western states, the list lengthens to include *Arctostaphylos uva-ursi* and *Baccharis pilularis* 'Twin Peaks.'

Ground cover succulents. To the surprise of many gardeners, succulents can make excellent small-space ground covers. Their effects under trees, along walks or among rocks can be dramatic. At the top of the list are the stonecrops (*Sedum* species). They come in a wide assortment of foliage forms and colors, many appearing to be in constant bloom. They are relatively undemanding, most are extremely hardy, and many have beautiful flowers. Familiarize yourself with the stonecrops at a local nursery. If they excite you, search out a specialist nursery to see all their possibilities.

Western gardeners should look for other colorful succulents, including the many species of *Lampranthus*. For ground covers with spectacular flowers, look to the very hardy sea pinks (*Armeria maritima*), various species of *Campanula*, *Phlox subulata* or the cinquefoil (*Potentilla* species). And western gardeners should not forget the brilliant *Osteospermum*, *Gazania* and *Arctotheca*.

Any discussion of ground covers must include English ivy. When kept within bounds (which can be difficult), it can be quite attractive. For different textures, take a look at the many varieties with interesting leaf shapes and colors.

Collection of ground cover succulents

Plant these in deep shade

While some plants tolerate degrees of shade, others such as those listed below require shade.

Botanical name	Common name
Adiantum pedatum	Maidenhair fern
Asarum species	Wild ginger
Athyrium goeringianum	Japanese painted fern
Convallaria majalis	Lily-of-the-valley
Galium odoratum	Sweet woodruff
Hosta species	Plantain lily
Oxalis oregana	Redwood sorrel
Pachysandra terminalis	Japanese pachysandra
Sarcococca ruscifolia	Fragrant sarcococca
Soleirolia soleirolii	Baby's tears
Vinca minor	Dwarf periwinkle
Viola odorata	Sweet violet

Tuck these into nooks or crannies

If you're not sure what to plant in a small corner, try one of these.

Botanical name	Common name
Arabis alpina	Mountain rock cress
Armeria maritima	Sea pink, thrift
Campanula species	Bellflower
Chamaemelum nobile	Chamomile
Dianthus 'Tiny Rubies'	Pinks
Epimedium grandiflorum	Barrenwort
Erodium chamaedryoides	Alpine geranium
Iberis sempervirens	Edging candytuft, evergreen candytuft
Lysimachia nummularia	Moneywort
Mentha requienii	Corsican mint
Veronica repens	Creeping speedwell

Use these in light traffic

Plant these between and around stepping stones and around patio paving.

Botanical name	Common name
Arenaria balearica	Corsican sandwort
Chamaemelum nobile	Chamomile
Glechoma hederacea	Ground ivy
Laurentia fluviatilis	Blue star creeper
Phyla nodiflora	Matgrass
Sagina subulata	Pearlwort, Irish moss
Thymus serpyllum	Lemon thyme, creeping thyme

Use these to drape, trail, and fill

They spill over low walls, trail down fences and grow to fill in every void. Some need occasional trimming.

Botanical name	Common name
Arctostaphylos uva-ursi	Kinnikinnick
Cotoneaster species	Cotoneaster (low growing kinds)
Euonymus fortunei	Wintercreeper
Hedera helix	English ivy
Pachysandra terminalis	Japanese spurge
Vinca major	Periwinkle
Vinca minor	Dwarf periwinkle

Campanula *(Campanula poscharskyana).*

Plantain lily *(Hosta lancifolia)*

Vines

It is unfortunate that more gardeners do not use more vines in their gardens. The nature of their growth, constantly climbing toward the sky and using space unoccupied by other plants, makes them ideal for gardens with limited growing area.

Vines are both functional and attractive landscape plants. They can cover a hot white wall with soft green foliage and, more often than not, provide seasonal flower color. Trained over an arbor, vines can even provide cooling summer shade.

But when selecting a vine, you have to be very careful. Most vines are fast growing; and some can fill a large trellis or cover a wall in one growing season. While this fast growth can be a blessing in most instances, it can lead to trouble if you ignore it. Keep pruning shears handy and use them fearlessly when they're needed. Overgrown vines can be a terrible nuisance, damaging structures and taking over other plants.

You should also realize that many vines require some type of support. Plants such as English ivy or *Euonymus* are clinging vines that can attach to anything, including walls and trellises.

Other vines either twine around objects or attach themselves by tendrils—these are the vines that need some type of support. Twining vines can climb a single wire. Tendrils need support across as well as up and down. Wire mesh or wood lattice work well in both cases. Left to their own devices, without support, many vines make good ground covers.

Trees make poor supports for climbing vines. As the vines grow higher, more and more leaf surface of the tree is shaded out. Many a tall tree has succumbed to vigorous growing vines.

Which vine? There are many excellent choices. You should base your selection on several factors. How fast does it grow? What exposure does it need? Does it have any special cultural requirements? Will it need support? And, of course, how hardy is it and is it evergreen or deciduous?

Clematis is a large family of mostly deciduous vines that climb with the aid of tendrils. Their blossoms are truly spectacular. They bloom from late spring to fall, depending upon the species, in beautiful shades of purple, blue, red, rose and white. The flowers come in many interesting shapes and sizes—some reaching 5 to 6 inches in diameter. Many are fragrant and the seed pods that follow the blossoms are shapely. Some of the favorites include the easy-to-grow sweet autumn clematis (*C. paniculata*) with fragrant white flowers and the spring-flowering pink anemone clematis (*C. montana rubens*).

Keep the roots and lower parts of the clematis vine cool and in the shade. A mulch is helpful. The flowering portion should be in full sun.

Two species of *Parthenocissus* are also valuable vines for foliage effects. The Virginia creeper (*P. quinquefolia*) and Boston ivy (*P. tricuspidata*) have attractive lobed leaves that turn brilliant orange or red in fall. Several varieties of each, some with variegated foliage, are available. But again, be warned that these are vigorous vines that attach to surfaces with small tendrils like suction cups. They can destroy wood sidings or chip away a wall's surface when removed. Keep them under control.

Winter creeper (Euonymus fortunei) is another excellent evergreen foliage vine especially valuable in cold climates. It clings to walls with tiny rootlets, is easy to control, and the small leaves result in quite a fine texture. It bears reddish-orange berries in fall. There are many varieties, not all of them climbing. Two of the best for walls are the big-leaf winter creeper (*E.f. vegata*) and the delicate *E. fortunei* 'Kewensis.'

For foliage plus edible fruit, you should consider the many varieties of grapes. They will cover a trellis quickly, provide sweet fall fruit, and beautiful fall color.

Grapes root very deeply if they can, although good grapes grow on a variety of soils. Improve very heavy clay with organic material. The soil should drain fairly quickly to prevent root damage. Grapes often do well on sloping or hilly ground because of exposure and air and water drainage. The vines must have moisture available at all times. A mulch will help ensure moist soil.

Wonderful fragrance is afforded by two other common vines, honeysuckle and wisteria.

Climbing hydrangea (*Hydrangea anomala petolaris*)

The honeysuckles are hardy semi-evergreen vines that climb with vigorous twining growth. The most popular form is Hall's honeysuckle *(Lonicera japonica 'Halliana')*, which is also often seen as a ground cover. Sweetly fragrant, white, trumpet shaped flowers bloom in late spring into summer and sometimes again in fall. Hall's honeysuckle forms a very thick vine and requires strong support.

The delicate look of the *Chinese wisteria (W. sinensis)* can be a bit misleading. It is a vigorous twining vine that needs strong support. Aside from this, it is one of the finest vines you can choose. Most varieties form beautiful long clusters of fragrant purple or lavender flowers in spring before the foliage unfolds. A white flowering form is also available. The soft green, divided leaves cast a very pleasant shade.

Wisterias require annual pruning to direct their growth and maximize flowering. When young, they benefit from an occasional light fertilizing. Otherwise, they flower best in infertile soil.

Climbing roses are a fine choice where a vine is needed to cover a fence or lattice. 'Don Juan' is a popular variety with double red fragrant flowers and attractive dark green foliage. Other good varieties include the scarlet flowered 'Blaze,' coral pink 'America,' dark red 'Red Fountain,' and daffodil yellow 'Golden Showers.' Keep in mind that climbing roses are still roses and need the same good care that bush types do.

Other spectacular flowering vines adaptable to small gardens include the climbing hydrangea *(H. anomala petiolaris)* and the trumpet creeper *(Campsis radicans)*. In mild regions of the West and South, make sure you consider the many forms of bougainvillea. Their flowering splendor is rarely equaled.

Five-leaf akebia *(A. quinata)* is a vine that combines interesting fruit with attractive deep green foliage. It is a twining vine that needs support but will thrive in sun or shade. The rather inconspicuous spring flowers are followed by purple sausage-like fruit in autumn. The five-fingered akebia benefits from annual pruning.

English ivy (Hedera helix) is probably the most famous vine in America. This very vigorous vine, which attaches to anything with rootlike holdfasts, is grown primarily for its foliage. Although most people recognize the common, very tenacious deep green form, few realize the wide assortment of leaf shapes and colors that can be found in its varieties. Look for beautiful forms like the small leafed 'Baltica' or the white edged 'Glacier.' All English ivies are easy to grow under a wide range of conditions, but take over quickly if not kept under control.

Annual vines. Finally, two annual vines are useful in small gardens. Sweet peas and morning glories are both exceptional flowers. Sweet peas bloom in a wide range of colors, are sweetly fragrant, and thrive in the cool months of spring and fall. Morning glories bloom in shades of red, white and blue, and thrive in summer heat. However, they are vigorous and reseed heavily. Use them with care.

Evergreen vines

All-season performers, these grow fast to make a screen. They can convert a bare fence into a hedge.

Botanical name	Common name
Bougainvillea species	Bougainvillea
Cissus species	Grape ivy
Clematis armandii	Evergreen clematis
Euonymus fortunei	Winter creeper
Ficus pumila	Creeping ficus
Gelsemium sempervirens	Evening trumpet flower, Carolina jessamine
Hedera helix	English ivy
Jasminum nitidum	Angel-wing jasmine
Lonicera japonica	Japanese honeysuckle
Polygonum aubertii	Silver lace vine
Rosa species	Climbing roses
Solanum jasminoides	Potato vine

Draping varieties of *Bougainvillea*.

Deciduous vines

Some of the hardiest vines are here. Also here are well-known vines that flower and fruit.

Botanical name	Common name
Actinidia chinensis	Kiwi berry
Akebia quinata	Five-leaf akebia
Celastrus scandens	American bittersweet
Clematis species	Clematis, vase vine
Hydrangea anomala	Climbing hydrangea
Parthenocissus tricuspidata	Boston ivy
Polygonum baldschuanicum	Bukhara fleece flower
Vitis species	Grape
Wisteria species	Wisteria

Annual vines

Quick and colorful, annual vines are favored problem-solvers. Besides fast cover, they can give summer shade for a greenhouse or patio.

Botanical name	Common name
Asarina erubescens	Creeping gloxinia
Cardiospermum halicacabum	Balloon vine
Centrosema virginianum	Butterfly pea
Clitoria ternatea	Pigeon-wings
Cobaea scadens	Cup-and-saucer vine
Cucurbita pepo ovifera	Field pumpkin, yellow-flowered gourds
Dolichos lablab	Hyacinth bean
Eccremocarpus scaber	Glory flower
Echinocystis lobata	Wild cucumber
Humulus japonicus	Japanese hop
Ipomoea species	Morning-glory
Lagenaria siceraria	White-flowered gourds
Lathyrus odoratus	Sweet pea
Luffa acutangula	Loofah, Dishcloth gourd
Phaseolus coccineus	Scarlet runner bean
Thunbergia alata	Black-eyed Susan vine
Tropaeolum majus	Garden nasturtium

Shade vines

Small-space gardens are commonly plagued by shade. If shade limits your choice of plants, try these vines.

Botanical name	Common name
Aristolochia durior	Dutchman's-pipe
Euonymus fortunei	Winter creeper
Gelsemium sempervirens	Evening trumpet flower, Carolina jessamine
Hydrangea anomala petiolaris	Climbing hydrangea
Parthenocissus species	Woodbine, Boston ivy, Virginia creeper
Schizophragma hydrangeoides	Japanese hydrangea vine
Thunbergia glandiflora	Blue trumpet vine
Trachelospermum jasminoides	Star jasmine

Perennials

A perennial, by definition, is a plant that lives on year to year. Its life cycle is not completed in one year as an annual's is, or in two years as a biennial's. Actually, trees, shrubs, vines, bulbs, and many ground covers are perennials.

Practically speaking, climate can also determine what is an annual or a perennial. In mild regions of the West and South, tender plants such as geraniums or chrysanthemums can live year to year without protection. In colder regions, these plants are treated as annuals, and new plants are put in the ground each spring.

In terms of small-space gardening, perennials is a catch-all category made up of valuable plants that don't fit nicely into the category of trees, shrubs, ground covers, vines, or annuals. It includes the flowering perennials, ferns, succulents, herbs and ornamental grasses.

Flowering perennials. In the traditional sense, these are the true perennials. European gardeners have long appreciated their value. The perennial border, with one plant or another always in bloom, is one of the most popular forms of gardening. The concept is simple: plant many types of herbacious perennials with different flowering seasons in one area.

In the small-space garden, you can either follow the lead of European gardeners and plant a perennial border, or you can follow many of the rules that apply to annuals: plant them in containers and bring them up front as they hit their peak, then pull them out (pot them up and save them) after they bloom.

The list of available perennials is a long one. Many of their names will be familiar to flower lovers. Which one you choose should depend on the plant's cultural requirements, hardiness, rapidity of growth, season of bloom and color of flower. Many perennials also have attractive foliage.

Some of the classic flowering perennials are the *Alyssum saxitile*, the large family of *Dianthus* (carnations, sweet william, pinks and more), the asters, chrysanthemums, geraniums, delphiniums, hibiscus, peonies, poppies, primrose, iberis and many others. Indeed, the world of flowering perennials offers infinite possibilities. Ask about them at your favorite nursery or garden center.

Ferns. Most people are familiar with the cool, forest feeling created by ferns. Among the most popular houseplants, ferns are also valuable as landscape plants. Ferns are the ultimate problem-solver for shady gardens. They are ideal for containers and can even be used as small-scale ground covers. And a good many ferns are hardy enough to survive cold winters.

Look for species of the wood fern (*Dryopteris*), the lady fern (*Athyrium*), and members of the *Matteuccia* family, to

103

name a few good ferns. In mild climates, the list grows longer to include the squirrel-foot fern (*Davallia trichomanoides*) and many others commonly thought of as houseplants.

In cold climates, try growing tender ferns in containers and moving them indoors in cold weather.

Flowering perennials that bloom in the shade

Some of these plants will grow best in sun but all will bloom in the shade.

Botanical name	Common name
Acanthus mollis	Bear's-breech
Aconitum species	Aconite, Monkshood
Astilbe species	Meadowsweet
Bergenia species	Bergenia
Campanula species	Bellflower
Convallaria majalis	Lily-of-the-valley
Dicentra spectabilis	Bleeding-heart
Helleborus species	Hellebore
Mertensia virginica	Bluebells, Roanoke-bells
Polygonatum multiflorum	Solomon's-seal
Primula species	Primrose
Pulmonaria species	Lungwort
Rehmannia elata	Rehmannia
Trillium species	Wake-robin, Birthroot
Trollius species	Globeflower
Vancouveria species	Vancouveria

Succulents With Beautiful flowers

Many of these succulents have attractive foliage besides beautiful flowers:

Botanical name	Common name
Adenium species	Adenium, Desert rose
Caralluma europaea	Caralluma
Chamaecereus sylvestri	Peanut cactus
Cleistocactus baumannii	Scarlet-bugler
Diplocyatha ciliata	Diplocyatha
Echinocereus cinerascens	Echinocereus
Echinocactus conglomeratus	Strawberry cactus
Hylocereus undatus	Night-blooming cereus, Queen-of-the-night
Mamillopis senilis	Mamillopsis
Notocactus haselbergii	Scarlet ball cactus
Pelargonium echinatum	Cactus geranium
Schlumbergia bridgesii	Christmas cactus
Selinicereus grandiflorus	Queen-of-the-night

Perennial succulents. Succulent lovers are in a world of their own. After being introduced to this large category of plants with varying forms, colors and textures, you'll see why. They go far beyond the heat-loving cactus and include some of the world's most spectacular flowering plants.

Herbs and spices. The only thing that comes close to

Many of the favorite herbs for cooking are easily grown in suspended gardens such as shown above.

matching the effects herbs and spices have on great foods is the results they can have in the garden. They're high quality ornamentals, perfectly suited for containers, can add spicy fragrance to the air; and they bring fresh herbs and spices to the kitchen.

Many herbs are easily started from seed and make relatively few demands from then on. Anise, basil, various mints, oregano, parsley, rosemary and thyme are just a few that will fit perfectly into the small-space garden. See pages 46-49 for more on growing herbs.

Ornamental grasses. For a unique texture, you might want to consider some of the ornamental grasses. Their effect can be quite dramatic; they're easy to grow, and many of their seed heads are valued for dried arrangements. Be cautioned, though: some ornamental grasses can spread by seed rather rapidly.

In addition to the ground cover grasses (page 98), some of the grasses to consider for small spaces are blue line or blue wild rye grass (*Elymus glaucus*), variegated moor grass (*Molinea caerulea*) and wild oats or spangle grass (*Chasmanthium latifolium*). Most are easily started from seed available from mail order houses dealing in perennials.

Annuals

There are many ways to use the colors of annuals. You can place the plants here and there, filling empty spaces with a pansy or a petunia or two. You can also use annuals to highlight other plants or garden features, to brighten up a shady corner with white impatiens or to call attention to a doorway with bright zinnias. Or you can be bold and boisterous, letting annual flowers be the theme, blending and matching, contrasting and aligning. Your small garden then becomes a wonderful world of color.

No garden should be without flower color. Annuals and flowering bulbs are the quickest and easiest way to get it.

Timing. The expert flower grower's goal is to have flowers blooming in the garden over the longest period possible. This is easily achieved with a little understanding of flowering timetables.

Most annuals classify themselves conveniently into those that bloom best in cool weather and those that bloom best in warm weather. The cool season types (pansies, violas, primrose) flower most vigorously in the cool months of spring and fall, and burn out in summer heat. In mild areas of the West and South, they may bloom all winter if planted in early fall. Warm season annuals (marigolds, petunias, zinnias) thrive in summer heat and quit flowering or die as the weather cools.

Knowing these cycles, you can plan for a long season of color. As cool season annuals are peaking in the spring, begin thinking of the warmer months ahead. Start seed of the warm season annuals or buy nursery 6-packs and plant them in 4-inch pots. They will be ready to bloom just as the cool season annuals are on their way out. If you live in an area of mild winters, start cool season annuals late in summer. In harder climates, germinate seeds indoors in winter so they're ready when the ground thaws in spring.

Another way to keep flowers in the garden for the longest period possible is by growing them in containers or hanging baskets. As one group moves past their prime, another group, ready to flower, is shifted into sight.

Which annual? Your choice is a wide one, especially if you shop in mail order catalogs. Flowering annuals are not only available in almost every color imaginable but in a variety of plant forms—from tall and erect to short and mounding, to low and spreading.

When grouping various annuals together, keep the low ones in front and the tall ones in back. Low-growing and spreading types are best for containers and hanging baskets. Keep the sun lovers in the sunny spots and those that thrive in the shade in sheltered areas.

For bright and summer heat, the most popular annuals are marigolds, petunias, and zinnias. Each has a multitude of available varieties.

Marigolds range in size from the tiny Petite series (6 to 8 inches) to larger varieties such as the Climax series, which grows from 24 to 36 inches high. Flower size, both singles and doubles, generally increases with the size of the variety and ranges from ¾ inch to 5 inches in diameter. Flower colors are mainly in shades and combinations of red, yellow and orange. Some of the excellent varieties include the bright yellow 'First Lady' (18 inches), 'Bolero' (8 inches), with gold and red bicolored flowers, and 'Spun Gold' (12 inches) with large gold flowers. Also consider the exceptionally heavy-flowering mule (triploid) marigolds such as 'Legal Gold.'

Petunias and zinnias come in a myriad of bright colors. Petunias are generally low (6 to 12 inches) and rather spreading, and come in either single or double flowering forms.

Flower types are distinguished as multiflora and grandifloras. Grandifloras usually have ruffled or fringed flowers. Although they have larger flowers and are vigorous growing, they do not produce as many flowers. Multifloras are more compact and have more, but smaller, smooth-edged flowers.

Favorite grandiflora varieties include the versatile Cascade series which is excellent for containers, hanging baskets, or draping over walls. Also look for bright red 'El Toro,' wine red 'Sugar Daddy,' and the bicolored 'Astro.'

Zinnias range from the 6 to 8 inch varieties such as 'Thumbelina' to the tall cut-flower types such as the Zenith series that reach 4 to 5 feet high. They come in many interesting flower shapes.

To keep zinnias looking their best, avoid wetting the foliage in late afternoon or early evening. That tends to encourage mildew. Another tip: Zinnias will flower longer and more profusely if spent flowers are picked before they become completely dry.

Fibrous begonias flower primarily in shades of red, pink and white, and range in size from 6 to 18 inches high. Foliage color also varies. Some are soft green, others have reddish bronze leaves. Popular green leafed varieties include 'Linda' (pink), 'Viva' (white) and 'Scarletta' (scarlet) with bronze foliage; 'Gin' (pink), 'Vodka' (red) and 'Whiskey' (white). Begonias can take more sun than impatiens.

Some annuals are grown more for their foliage than for their flowers. Two standouts are coleus and dusty millers. Coleus thrive in the shade and offer a large variety of leaf colors and patterns to choose from. Dusty millers have silvery gray foliage as well as bright yellow flowers in spring or summer. They grow best in hot sun and are excellent when used to highlight other plants.

You can't mention annuals for highlighting without including sweet alyssum. It forms a low—4 to 6 inch—carpet of white, pink or purple flowers. Used as a low edging in front of other annuals, sweet alyssum brings other flower colors to new levels of excitement.

For the cool months of spring and fall, look to pansies

and violas for the longest period of color. Their flowers look similar, but those of pansies are much larger. Viola flowers are smaller but more profuse. Both come in a wide range of colors and grow best in full sun but will take light shade. 'Imperial Blue' and 'Imperial Orange' are excellent pansy varieties. 'Johnny Jump-up' is a long-time favorite viola in purple and yellow.

While considering the annuals, take a close look at the geraniums and dianthus. Flower breeders have made great strides in introducing spectacular varieties of each.

Which bulb? Flowering bulbs can also brighten up small gardens with spectacular colors. Ideally planted in fall, they can provide color in any season (crocus and freesia can pop up through snow) and can be forced in containers for indoor bloom or early outdoor flowers.

Growing bulbs in containers is an ideal plan for the small-space gardener. After the flowers are spent, the containers can be moved out of sight where the foliage can store energy for next year's bloom. Then fresh color can be brought in.

Another nice way to handle bulbs is to plant them under ground covers or annuals. The blossoms from the bulbs can contrast dramatically with other foliage or flowers. Daffodils work very well in this type of situation.

Whenever bulbs are mentioned, most people immediately think of daffodils and tulips. While the merits of these two fine plants are undoubtedly justified, to think of them as the only choices would be unfortunate. There are many other excellent bulbs (many are technically corms, tubers or rhizomes). Be sure you consider the fine forms of anemone, cannas, gladiolus, lilies, agapanthus, tuberous begonias and iris. They are truly some of the most spectacular flowering plants in the world.

Annuals for full sun

These are some of the best plants for color where the full effect of the sun is felt. They are the favorite summer annuals.

Amaranthus hybridus	Green amaranthus; reddish foliage and flower spikes
Artemisia stellerana	Dusty-miller; felty-white leaves and yellow flowers
Callistephus chinensis	China aster; many colors
Celosia cristata	Cockscomb or feathered amaranth; shades of red, white, yellow and purples
Centaurea cyanus	Bachelor button or cornflower; usually blue but also purples and pink
Cosmos species	Cosmos; dark reds, yellows, pink, orange
Gaillardia x grandiflora	Blanket flower; good yellows, reds and orange
Gazania ringens	Gazania; yellows and oranges
Helianthus annuus	Sunflower; yellows
Petunia x hybrida	Petunia; many colors

Portulaca grandiflora	Moss rose, portulaca; bright colors
Salvia species	Salvia; scarlet reds
Tagetes species	Marigold; yellow, oranges and red browns
Verbena x hybrida	Verbena; pink, red, white, yellowish, blue, purple, and combinations
Zinnia elegans	Zinnia; many colors and varieties

Annuals that drape or trail

Virtually all annuals can be grown in containers but the following will gracefully spill over edges and borders. Ideal for hanging baskets.

Browallia species	Bush violet; white, lilac and purples
Dianthus barbatus	Sweet William; white, pink, rose, reds, purples and combinations
Gazania ringens leucolaena	Trailing gazania; yellow
Lobelia erinus	Lobelia; blue or violet
Lobularia maritima	Sweet alyssum; white
Pelargonium peltatum	Ivy geranium; reds and whites
Petunia x hybrida	Petunia; many colors
Portulaca grandiflora	Moss rose; many colors
Sanvitalia procumbens	Creeping zinnia; dark centers, yellow to orange petals
Thunbergia alata	Black-eyed Susan vine; dark center with creamy, white or purple throat
Viola tricolor	Johnny-jump-up; yellows, purples and violet blue

Annuals for shade

The following annuals prefer shaded locations and serve to brighten them with colorful flowers or foliage. They are commonly available as bedding plants from your local nursery.

Begonia species	Begonia; good reds and whites
Browallia species	Bush violet; white, lilac, and purples
Calceolaria crenatiflora	Pocketbook flower; many colors
Coleus x hybridus	Flame nettle; colorful foliage
Impatiens species	Impatiens; many colors
Mimulus x hybridus	Monkey flower; many colors
Myosotis scorpioides	Forget-me-not; blue with yellow, pink or white center
Pelargonium peltatum	Ivy-leaf geranium; reds and whites
Primula species	Primrose; many colors
Senecio x hybridus	Cineraria; many colors but no yellows
Viola tricolor	Johnny-jump-up; combinations of yellows, purples and violet blue
Viola x wittrockiana	Pansy; many colors

Sources

One book can hold only so much information. The pages that follow are designed to help you get more. All of these publications and suppliers offer something of interest to small-space gardeners. Catalogs can be as informative as a good book and a delight to peruse.

Books

Bonsai Techniques
John Yoshio Naka
Published for the Bonsai
    Institute of California
by Dennis-Landman Co.,
Santa Monica, CA

Lynn R. Perry,
Bonsai: Trees and Shrubs
The Ronald Press Co.,
New York, NY

Gardening in Containers
Small Gardens for Small
    Spaces
Brooklyn Botanic Garden
    Publications
Brooklyn Botanic Garden
1000 Washington Ave.
Brooklyn, NY 11225

**Cornell Peat-Lite Mixes for
    Commercial Plant
    Growing**
Information Bulletin 43
New York State College of
    Agriculture
Ithaca, NY 14850

Dwarf Fruit Trees
by Lawrence Southwick
Garden Way Publishing
Charlotte, VT 05445

**How to Grow More
    Vegetables Than You
    Ever Thought Possible
    on Less Land Than
    You Can Imagine**
by John Jeavons
Ecology Action of the
    Midpeninsula
2225 El Camino Real
Palo Alto, CA 94306

The Mini-Bonsai Hobby
Tei'ichi Katayama
Japan Publications, Inc.
Tokyo, Japan

New Western Garden Book
by the Editors of Sunset
    Books and Sunset
    Magazine
Lane Publishing Co.
Menlo Park, CA 94025

Ortho Book Series
All About Ground Covers
*All About Growing Fruits &
    Berries*
All About Vegetables
*Container & Hanging
    Gardens*
*Do-it-yourself Garden
    Construction Know-How*
*How to Build & Use
    Greenhouses*
*How to Design & Build
    Decks & Patios*
*The Facts of Light About
    Indoor Gardening*
The World of Trees
12-Month's Harvest
*Wood Projects for the
    Garden*
Ortho Books
575 Market Street
San Francisco, CA 94105

The Small Garden
by John Brookes
Macmillan Publishing Co.
866 Third Ave.
New York, NY 10022

**The U.C. System for
    Producing Healthy
    Container-Grown Plants**
Manual 23
Agricultural Publications
University of California,
    Berkeley
Berkeley, CA 94720

**Wyman's Gardening
    Encyclopedia**
by Donald Wyman
Macmillan Publishing Co.
866 Third Ave.
New York, NY 10022

Your Private World
by Thomas Church
Chronicle Books
870 Market Street
Suite 915
San Francisco, CA 94102

Plant societies

When you become interested in some particular aspect of horticulture, joining an appropriate plant society is one of the best ways to further your knowledge. The information in their bulletins is first hand and up-to-date.

**African Violet Society of
    America, Inc.**
Box 1326
Knoxville, TN 37901
Membership $6.00 per year
    includes
African Violet Magazine
    (5 times per year)

**American Bonsai Society,
    Inc.**
228 Rosemont Ave.
Erie, PA 16505
Membership $10.00 per year
    includes
Bonsai Journal (quarterly)
*Abstracts (interim monthly
    newsletter)* library book
    rental, film and slide pro-
    gram rentals, members
    discount book purchasing
    service.

**American Orchid
    Society, Inc.**
Botanical Museum of
    Harvard University
Cambridge, MA 02138
Membership $15.00 per year
    includes
*American Orchid Society
    Bulletin (monthly)*

**American Rock Garden
    Society**
Office of the Secretary
3 Salisbury Lane
Malvern, PA 19355
16 regional chapters.
Membership $7.00 per year
    includes
*Bulletin of the American
    Rock Garden Society
    (quarterly)*

Bonsai Clubs International
445 Blake Street
Menlo Park, CA 94025
Membership $7.50 per year
    includes
*Bonsai Magazine (10 times
    yearly)*

**Bonsai Society of Greater
    New York, Inc.**
P.O. Box 343
New Hyde Park, NY 11040
Corresponding membership
    $9.00 per year; Interna-
    tional corres. memb.
    $10.00 per year; Active
    membership $12.00 per
    year.
Bonsai Bulletin (quarterly)

Bromeliad Society, Inc.
P.O. Box 3279
Santa Monica, CA 90403
Membership $10.00 per year
    includes
*Bromeliad Journal (6 times
    yearly)*

**Cactus and Succulent
    Society of America, Inc.**
P.O. Box 3010
Santa Barbara, CA 93105
Membership $12.50 per year
    includes
*Cactus and Succulent
    Journal (bimonthly)*

Herb Society of America
300 Massachusetts Avenue
Boston, MA 02115
1300 members; units in
    many states
The Herbarist (annually)

**Indoor Light Gardening
    Society of America, Inc.**
423 Powell Drive
Bay Village, OH 44140
30 regional chapters.
Membership $5.00 per year
    includes
Light Garden (bimonthly)

National Fuchsia Society
c/o Bonita Doan, Dept. DH
774 Forest Loop Drive
Point Hueneme, CA 93041
Membership $6.00 per year
    includes
The Fuchsia Fan (monthly)

House plants and indoor growing supplies

Alberts & Merkel
Brothers, Inc.
2210 S. Federal Highway
Boynton Beach, FL 33435

Catalog and price list $.50.

Arant's Exotic Greenhouses
1873 S. Shady Crest Rd.
Bessemer, AL 35020

Specializes in ferns,
bromeliads and orchids.
Catalog $1.50.

Edelweiss Gardens
54 Robb-Allentown Road
Robbinsville, NJ 08691

Large collection of tropical
plants. Price list $.35.

Fisher Greenhouses
Linwood, NJ 08221

Variety of supplies for
indoor gardeners.
Catalog $.50.

Greenland Flower Shop
Route 1, Box 52 (Stormstown)
Port Matilda, PA 16870

Wide variety of rare
houseplants. Catalog $.30.

Greenlife Gardens
Route 3, Box 613
Griffin, GA 30223

Wide variety of exotic plants.
Price list $.30.

Harborcrest Nurseries
4634 W. Saanich Road
Victoria, BC V8Z 3G8, Canada

Hundreds of kinds of
houseplants. Catalog $.25.

Hewston Green
Box 3115
Seattle, WA 98199

Miniatures as well as indoor
trees and shrubs. Price list
$.50.

Jerry Horne
10195 S.W. 70th Street
Miami, FL 33173

Specializes in rare exotics.
Free catalog.

International Growers
Exchange, Inc.
Box 397-V
Farmington, MI 48024

Very large collection of
tropicals. Catalog $3.00.

Kartuz Greenhouses
92 Chestnut Street
P.O. Box 115
Wilmington, MA 01887

Specializes in rare plants,
gesneriads and begonias.
Catalog $1.00.

Kuaola Farms, Ltd.
Box 4038
Hilo, HI 96720

Bare-root and potted
Anthurium *plants. Free*
price list.

Lauray of Salisbury
Undermountain Road
Route 41
Salisbury, CT 06068

Rare gesneriads, begonias,
fuchsias and succulents.
Catalog $.85.

Lehua Anthurium Nursery
80 Kokea Street
Hilo, HI 96720

Unusual varieties of many
tropicals. Send stamped
envelope for price list.

Loyce's Flowers
Route 2, Box 11
Granbury, TX 76048

Wide selection of hoyas.
Price list $.50.

Merry Gardens
Box 595
Camden, ME 04843

Long list of many kinds of
indoor plants. Price list
$.50.

Walter F. Nicke
19 Columbia Turnpike
Hudson, NY 12534

Many garden specialities,
unique items.

Shadow Lawn Nursery
637 Holly Land
Plantation, FL 33317

Both plants and seeds of
many indoor plants
available. Specialize in
variegated and unusual
foliage plants. Catalog $.30.

Small-Space Fruits

Ask your local nurseryman for the fruit plants you are looking for. If he cannot supply them, the mail-order suppliers listed here probably can.

Many of the catalogs from these suppliers of dwarf fruit and other home-garden fruit plants are the equivalent of a good garden book. They contain excellent reference material.

Adams Country Nursery &
Fruit Plants
Aspers, PA 17304

Free catalog.

Andrews Nursery Co.
Andrews Road
Faribault, MN 55021

Bountiful Ridge
Nurseries, Inc.
Box 250
Princess Anne, MD 21853

Free catalog.

Bowers Berry Nursery
94959 Highway 99E
Junction City, OR 97448

Bunting's Nurseries
P.O. Box 306
Selbyville, DE 19975

Free catalog.

Burgess Seed and Plant Co.
P.O. Box 82
Galesburg, MI 49053

Ask for the special catalog
for small-space gardeners.
Free catalog.

Columbia Basin Nursery
Box 458
Quincy, WA 98828

Free catalog.

Dean Foster Nurseries
Route 2
Hartford, MI 49257

Free catalog.

Grootendorst Nurseries
10603 Clevland Ave.
Barota, MI 49101

Specialists in dwarf
Malling and Merton
apple rootstocks.

Heath's Nursery, Inc.
P.O. Box 438
Quincy, WA 98828

Free catalog.

Hilltop Orchards &
Nurseries
Route #2
Hartford, MI 49057

Free catalog.

Ison's Nursery & Vineyard
Brooks, GA 30205

Grape specialists.

Kelly Brothers
Nurseries, Inc.
Dansville, NY 14437

Free catalog.

Lawson's Nursery
Route 1, Box 61
Ball Ground, GA 30107

Over 100 varieties of
old-fashioned apples.
Free catalog.

Henry Leuthardt
Nurseries, Inc.
East Moriches
Long Island, NY 11940

Specializes in espalier-
trained fruit trees.

Mayo Nurseries
Route 14
Lyons, NY 14489

Many varieties of dwarf and
semidwarf apples.

New York State Fruit Testing
Cooperative Association
Geneva, NY 14456

Membership fee of $5.00.
Free information bulletin.

Rayner's Brothers, Inc.
Salisbury, MD 21801

Free catalog.

Southmeadow Fruit Gardens
2363 Tilbury Place
Birmingham, MI 48009

Wide collection of fruit tree
varieties, old, new and
rare. Catalog, 112 pages,
costs $5.00.

Stark Brothers Nursery
Louisiana, MO 63353

Free catalog.

Dave Wilson Nursery
4306 Santa Fe Ave.
Hughson, CA 95326

Bonsai

The art of emulating nature known as bonsai is becoming more popular in western countries. If you are interested, here are sources of further information and supplies.

International Bonsai
412 Pinnacle Road
Rochester, NY 14623
New and up-to-date magazine

Bonsai International
Official publication of Bonsai
  Clubs International
P.O. Box 2098
Sunnyvale, CA 94087

Keith Scott's
Dwarfed Tree Nursery
17771 Snyder Road
Chagrin Falls, OH 44022

Modern Plant
  Technology, Inc.
Dept. 1, Route 1, Box 110
Purcellville, VA 22132

Greer Gardens
1280 Goodpasture
  Island Road
Eugene, OR 97401

Tosh Bonsai Nursery
1020 Weeks Street
East Palo Alto, CA 94303

Miniature landscapes

Plants for trough gardens may be hard to find. Below are listed nurseries offering a wide variety of rare and unusual plants suitable for troughs and other kinds of miniature gardens.

Alpenglow Gardens
13328 King George Highway
Surrey, BC V3T 2T6, Canada
Catalog, $1.00.

Brimfield Gardens Nursery
3109 Main Street
Rocky Hill, CT 06067
Catalog, $1.00.

Carroll Gardens
444 East Main Street
P.O. Box 310
Westminster, MD 21157
Free catalog.

The Cummins Garden
22 Robertsville Road
Marlboro, NJ 07746
Catalog, $.50.

Lamb Nurseries
101 E. Sharp Avenue
Spokane, WA 99202
Free catalog.

Laura's Collectors' Garden
5136 South Raymond Street
Seattle, WA 98118
Write for information.

Palette Gardens
26 West Zion Hill Road
Quakertown, PA 18951
Catalog, $.50.

The Plant Farm
11811 Northeast 73
Kirkland, WA 98033

Rakestraw's Gardens
G-3094
South Term
Burton, MI 48529
Catalog, $.50.

The Rock Garden
Route 2
Litchfield, ME 04350
Catalog, $.50.

Siskiyou Rare Plant Nursery
2825 Cummings Road
Medford, OR 97501
Catalog, $.50.

Joel W. Spingarn
1535 Forest Avenue
Baldwin, NY 11510
Catalog, $.50.

Wildwood Gardens
14488 Rock Creek Road
Chardon, OH 44024
Catalog, $.50.

Hydroponics

This is the art of growing plants without soil in a nutrient solution. Since no soil is necessary, hydroponic gardens can be anywhere—indoors, balcony or patio. Most of these suppliers offer informative catalogs.

Aqua-Ponics
22135 Ventura Blvd.
Woodland Hills, CA 91364

Continental Nutri-Culture
P.O. Box 6751
Lubbock, TX 79413

Earth Products
P.O. Box 4360
Pasadena, CA 91106

Eco Enterprises
2821 N.E. 55th
Seattle, WA 98105

Family Farms
9310 Willowview
Houston, TX 77080

Home Hydroponic Systems
90 Earlton Road
Agincourt, Ontario M1T 2R6
Canada

Homeland Industries, Inc.
95 Evergreen Avenue
Brooklyn, NY 11206

Hydroculture, Inc.
P.O. Box 1655
Glendale, AZ 85311

Hydro-Fresh Farm
P.O. Box 511
San Martin, CA 95046

Hydro-Gardens Inc.
P.O. Box 9707
Colorado Springs, CO 80932

Hydroponic Greenhouse
P.O. Box 336
Trona, CA 93562

Pacific Aquaculture
3A Gate 5 Road
Sausalito, CA 94965

Sunlan Greenhouse
P.O. Box 1526
519 E. College Street
Murfreesboro, TN 37130

Verti-Garden, Inc.
P.O. Box "C"
Sealy, TX 77474

Vegetable seed catalogs

Gardeners use catalogs such as these to track down varieties recommended by garden books and agriculture experiment stations. Also, catalogs are usually the first to offer the new or unusual.

Burgess Seed & Plant Co.
Box 2000
Galesburg, MI 49053

W. Atlee Burpee Co.
Philadelphia, PA 19132,
Clinton, IA 52732 or
Riverside, CA 92502

DeGiorgi Co., Inc.
Council Bluffs, IA 51501

J. A. Demonchaux Co.
225 Jackson
Topeka, KS 66603

Farmer Seed & Nursery Co.
Fairbault, MN 55021

Henry Field Seed and
  Nursery Co.
407 Sycamore St.
Shenandoah, IA 51601

Grace's Gardens
100 Autumn Lane
Hackettstown, NJ 07840

Gurney Seed & Nursery Co.
1448 Page St.
Yankton, SD 57078

Joseph Harris Co.
Moreton Farm
Rochester, NY 14624

H.G. Hastings Co.
Box 4088
Atlanta, GA 30302

Nichols Garden Nursery
1190 No. Pacific Highway
Albany, OR 97321

George W. Park
  Seed Co., Inc.
Greenwood, SC 29646

Stokes Seeds
Box 548 Main Post Office
Buffalo, NY 14240 or
St. Catherine's
Ontario, Canada

Lighting systems

Gardening with artificial light is the main interest of many small-space gardeners. Fluorescent and other growth-promoting light sources can make a garden bloom indoors. Some suppliers of light gardening equipment are:

Duro-Lite Lamps, Inc.
Duro-Lite Dept. OB
Fair Lawn, NJ 07410

Plant growth lamps.

Duro-Test Corporation
2331 Kennedy Blvd.
North Bergen, NJ 07047

*Fluorescent and
incandescent bulbs.*

Environment One
2773 Balltown Road
P.O. Box 773
Schenectady, NY 12301

Plant growth chambers.

Fluorescent Tube Service
13107 South Broadway
Los Angeles, CA 90061

Bulbs, lamps and fixtures.

General Electric
   Company
Lamp Division
Noble Rd.
Cleveland, OH 44112

*Incandescent and
fluorescent lamps.*

JD-21 Lighting Systems
1840 130th N.E.
Bellevue, WA 98005

*High-output fluorescent and
HID systems.*

Sylvania Electric
   Products, Inc.
60 Boston St.
Salem, MA 01971

*Fluorescent fixtures, bulbs
and tubes.*

Tube Craft, Inc.
1311 West 80th St.
Cleveland, OH 44102

Light units, trays and timers.

Westinghouse Electric
   Corporation
Lamp Division
1 Westinghouse Plaza
Bloomfield, NJ 07003

All types of fluorescent lamps.

Verta-A-Ray Corporation
615 Front St.
Toledo, OH 43605

Plant lights and stands.

Urban self-sufficiency

Integral Urban House (1516 5th St., Berkeley, CA 94710) is a combination of some of the oldest and newest technologies, all coordinated to demonstrate how to be self-sufficient in food and energy on a typical urban lot.

The project is sponsored by the Farallon Institute and serves as an information clearing-house on subjects such as solar energy, aquaculture, home and community gardening, pest control and even bee keeping.

An introductory booklet is available for $3.

Greenhouses

For city-dwellers, deck greenhouses may be the only gardening possibility. Renters may build a mobile greenhouse that can be easily taken apart and reassembled elsewhere.

Prefabricated units or components for building your own greenhouse may be secured from these suppliers:

Aluminum
   Greenhouses, Inc.
14615 Lorain Avenue
Cleveland, OH 44111

Feather Hill Industries
Box 41
Zenda, WI 53195

Hansen Weather-Port
313 North Taylor
Gunnison, CO 81230

Ickes-Braun Glasshouses
P.O. Box 147
Deerfield, IL 60015

Lord and Burnham
Irvington, NY 10533

National Greenhouse
   Company
P.O. Box 100
Pana, IL 62557

J.A. Nearing Company
10788 Tucker Street
Beltsville, MD 20705

Sturdi-Built
   Manufacturing Co.
11304 S.W. Boones
   Ferry Road
Portland, OR 97219

Texas Greenhouse Company
2717 St. Louis Avenue
Fort Worth, TX 76110

Community gardens

Learning about growing your own food on a shared basis is a very rewarding experience. If some of these ideas interest you, write to the organizations listed below for more information.

California Council for
   Community Gardening
P.O. Box 1715
Los Gatos, CA 95030

*Dedicated to serving
persons, groups or
agencies interested in
community gardening in
California.*

Community Gardening in
   California
By Rosemary Menninger
Office of Appropriate
   Technology
1530 10th Street
Sacramento, CA 95814

*Free for California residents.
Available out-of-state for
$1.50. Newsletter, **California
Green**, available (to Califor-
nians only) through same
office.*

Gardens for All
Box 371
Shelburne, VT 05482

*Nationwide promoters of
community gardening and
an information clearing-
house.*

Growing with Community
   Gardens
by Mary Lee Coe
The Countryman Press
Taftsville, VT 05073

*Very helpful book with
detailed information for
both organizers and
gardeners. Diagrams of
sample gardens.*

Organizing Neighborhood
   Gardens for Your
   Community
University of New
   Hampshire
Durham, NH 03824

Index

A

Abelia, 97
Abies balsamea, 92
Acer, 90
    ginnala, 90, 93
    palmatum, 51, 60, 90
Acclimatized plants, 68
African sumac, 94
Ageratum houstonianum, 52
Air pollution, 56, 57
Air space in soil, 16
Ajuga reptans, 98
Akebia, 102
Albizia julibrissin, 40
Alyssum saxitile, 103
American Association of Botanical Gardens and Arboreta, 6
Amur maple, 90, 93
Annuals, 89, 105-107
    vines, 102, 103
Apple trees, fence of, 81
Apricots, 82
Arbors, 82
Arborvitae, 93
Arbutus unedo, 94
Arctostaphylos uva-ursi, 22, 99
Arctotheca, 99
Armeria maritima, 99
Artificial lights, 69
Asarum caudatum, 50, 51
Asters, 103
Athyrium, 103
    goeringianum 'Pictum', 51
Aucuba japonica, 51, 60
Australian willow, 94

B

Baccharis, 99
Bailey, L. H., 5
Balcony gardens, 11, 54, 55, 60-63
Balsam fir, 92
Barberries, 96, 99
Barrenwort, 51
Basil, 46
Beets, 48, 76
Begonias, 88, 106
    semperflorens, 52
Bellflower, 51, 99, 100
Berberis, 96, 99
Berries, 80
Big blue liriope, 99
Blue fescue, 99
Bonsai, 12, 13, 24-27
    mame, 13, 26
    plants adaptable to, 25
    and sideyards, 39
    sources of, 110
Boston fern, 68
Boston ivy, 101
Bougainvillea, 12, 102
Boxwood. *See* Buxus

Brassaia actinophylla, 68
Brick patios, 34, 35
Browallia, 52
Bugleweed, 98
Bulbs, growing, 106
Burford holly, 96
Buxus, 22, 97
    microphylla japonica, 22
    sempervirens, 27

C

Cabbage, 76
Caladium, 98
Callery pear, 85, 90
Camellia, 96
    sasanqua, 97
Campanula, 51, 99, 100
Campsis radicans, 102
Cane berries, 82
Cantaloupe, 76
Carrots, 48, 76
Cattleya orchids, 7
Cercis canadensis, 90, 91
Chaenomeles, 96
Chamaecyparis, 92
Chamaemelum nobile, 98
Chamomile, 98
Cherries, 94
Chinese wisteria, 102
Chionanthus virginicus, 91
Chives, 47, 76
Cilantro, 47
Cinquefoil, 99
City gardens, 53
Clay pots, 14
Clematis, 101
Climbing plants, 22
    roses, 102
Cobaea scandens, 22
Cold climate trees, 94
Coleus, 52, 106
Color
    in shade, 52
    trees for, 94
Community gardens, 86, 87
    sources for, 111
Concrete patios, 36
Containers, 13-19
    apples in, 81, 82
    fruit plants in, 80, 81
    and kitchen gardens, 46-49
    shrubs for, 97
    soils for, 16-19
    and vegetables, 75
Contest winners, 6
Corn, 76
Cornell peat-lite mix, 17
Cornus, 91, 92, 95
    florida, 51, 91, 92
Cotoneasters, 60, 96, 99
    microphyllus, 22
Crabapple, 94
Cranberry cotoneaster, 99
Crannies, plants for, 100
Crape myrtle, 94
Crataegus, 91
Creeping cotoneaster, 99
Cryptomeria japonica, 92, 93
Cucumber, 77
Cup-and-saucer vine, 22
Currants, 80

D

Daffodil, 105
Daphne, 96
    odora, 51
Dark corners, plants for, 70, 100
Davallia trichomanoides, 104
Deciduous vines, 103
Decks, 55, 64-67
Design of garden, 8
Dianthus, 103
Dieffenbachia, 68
Dodonaea viscosa 'Purpurea', 44
Dogwood. *See* Cornus
Drainage, 16
Draping plants, 22, 100
    annuals, 107
Dryopteris, 51, 103
Dwarf trees, 80, 81, 85

E

Eggplant, 77
Elaeagnus angustifolia, 60
English hawthorn, 91
English holly, 91
English ivy, 22, 98, 101, 102
English yew, 22
Entryways, 31-33
Epimedium, 51
Eriobotrya deflexa, 23
Espalier, 13, 22, 23
    fruit trees, 81
    and sideyards, 40
Eucalyptus, 93
Euonymus, 96, 99, 101
    fortunei, 22, 51, 97, 99, 101
Evergreens, 92
    vines, 102
Evergreen cotoneaster, 99
Evergreen pear, 90, 91, 93

F

False cypress, 92
Fatsia japonica, 69
Fences for privacy, 43
Ferns, 103, 104
Fern pine, 93
Fertilizing plants, 68
    house gardens, 69
    synthetic soil mix, 19
Festuca glauca, 99
Ficus
    benjamina, 68
    microcarpa, 93, 94
Figs, 82
Fire thorn, 13, 23
Flowers
    perennials, 103, 104
    shrubs for, 96, 97
    succulents with, 104
Fluorescent light, 69
Forget-me-not, 52

Forsythia, 96
    ovata, 60
    suspensa, 22
Fragaria chiloensis, 98
Fragrant small trees, 95
French marigold, 107
Fringe tree, 91
Fruit trees, 22, 23
    for landscape use, 84
    sources of, 109
Fruits, 80-85

G

Gardenia, 96
Garlic, 47
Gazania, 99
Ginger, wild, 50, 51
Glossy privet, 93
Grandifloras, 105
Grapes, 82, 85
Grasses, ornamental, 104
Grejera parviflora, 94
Ground covers, 89, 98-100

H

Halesia carolina, 91
Hawthorns, 91
Heating patios, 36
Hedera helix, 22, 98, 101, 102
Hedge maple, 90
Hedges, 82
Hemlocks, 44, 93
Herbs, 46-48, 104
Holly. *See* Ilex
Honeysuckles, 102
Hopseed bush, 44
Hosta, 51, 100
Hydrangea, 96, 101, 102
    anomala petiolaris, 102
Hypericum, 98
Hypertufa, 28

I

Ilex, 60, 94, 97
    aquifolium, 91
    cornuta 'Burfordii', 96
    latifolia, 13, 23, 60
    noise, reduction of, 44
Impatiens walleriana, 52
Indian laurel, 93, 94
Indoor gardens, 55, 68-71
Ipomoea purpurea, 22, 102
Irish moss, 99

J

Jacaranda acutifolia, 94
Japanese flowering cherry, 90
Japanese honeysuckle, 22
Japanese laurel, 51, 60
Japanese maple, 90
Japanese privet, 93
Japanese snowbell, 94

Japanese style garden, 8
Jasminum, 96
Juniperus, 97, 99
 horizontalis, 22

K
Kinnikinick, 22, 99
Kitchen gardens, 31,
 46-49
Koelreuteria paniculata,
 94
Korean stewartia, 94

L
Lagerstroemia indica, 94
Lampranthus, 99
Landscaping
 with fruits, 84, 85
 with shrubs, 97
Laurus nobilis, 93
Lettuce, 48, 77
Light, artificial, 69
Lily-of-the-valley,
 51, 97
Lingustrum lucidum, 93
Lippia, 99
Liriope muscari, 99
Lobelia erinus, 52
Lonicera japonica,
 22, 102
Loquat, 23
Luster-leaf holly, 13

M
Magnolias, 91
 grandiflora, 23
Malus, 94
Mame bonsai, 13, 26
Maple. *See* Acer
Maranta leuconeura, 68
Marigolds, 105
'Max Graf' rose, 22
Maytenus boaria, 94
Mild climates, trees for,
 93, 94
Miniature plants, 10
 trees, 95
Mobile homes, 31,
 42-45
Mondo grass, 96, 98, 99
Monstera deliciosa, 69
Morning glories, 22, 102
Mountain pine, 92
Multiflora, 105
Myosotis sylvatica, 52

N
Narcissus, 105
Nectarines, 82
Needled evergreens, 92
Nephrolepis exaltata
 Bostoniensis', 68
Nicotiana, 52
Noise, plants to reduce,
 44
North balcony, 60
Norway maple, 90

O
Olea europaea, 93
Olive tree, 93
Onions, 77
Ophiopogon japonicus,
 96, 98, 99
Oregano, 47
Osmanthus, 96
Osteospermum, 99
Oxalis oregana, 50, 51
Oxydendrum arboreum,
 94

P
Paper plant, 69
Parsley, 47
Parthenocissus, 22, 101
Pathways, 8, 43
Patios, 31, 34-37
Paving, plants for around,
 100
Peaches, 82
Pears. *See* Pyrus
Peas, 78
Peiris japonica, 97
Peppers, 78
Perennials, 89, 103, 104
Petunias, 105
Phlox subulata, 99
Photinia, 97
Phyla nodiflora, 99
Picea, 93
Pieris japonica, 51
Pinus mugo, 92
 sylvestris, 60
Pittosporum, 97
 eugenoides, 40
 tobira, 69
Plantain lily, 51, 100
Plums, 82
Podocarpus, 51, 93
Populus alba, 94
Potatoes, 78
Potentilla, 99
Prayer plant, 68
Primroses, 50, 51
Primula polyantha, 50,
 51
Privacy, fences for, 43
Prunus, 93, 94
 cerasifera, 92
 serrulata, 90, 92
Pumpkin, 78
Purpleleaf plums, 94
Pyracantha coccinea, 13
 , 23
Pyrus, 85, 90, 91
 kawakamii, 40, 93

Q
Quince, 96

R
Raised beds, 13, 20, 21
Redbuds, 90, 91
Rhamnus, 44
Rhododendron, 51
Rhus lancea, 94
Rooftop gardens, 7, 11,
 55-59
Rosemary, 47, 99
Rosmarinus officinalis
 'Prostratus', 22
Russian olive, 60

S
Saburomaru, Toshio, 25
Sage, 48
Sagina subulata, 99
Salvia splendens, 52
Sapphire flower, 52
Sarcocca ruscifolia, 51
Sasanqua camellia, 97
Schefflera, 68
Scotch moss, 99
Sedum, 99
Shade, 30, 50-53
 annuals for, 107
 and perennials, 104
 plants for, 100
 and rooftops, 56
 vines for, 103
Shrubs, 89, 96, 97
Sideyards, 31, 38-41
Silverbells, 91
Skimmia japonica, 51
Small-Space Gardening
 Contest, 5, 6
Soil for containers, 16-19
Soil mixes, weight of, 57
Solarium, 68
Sources, 108-111
Southern magnolia, 91
Spinach, 48
Spindle trees, 97
Spruces, 93
Squash, 78
Stepping stones, plants
 for around, 100
Stewartia koreana, 94
Strawberries as ground
 cover, 84, 85
Style of garden, 8
Styrax japonicus, 94
Succulents, 99, 104
Sunlight
 and decks, 66
 and house gardens, 68
 and north-facing
 balcony, 60
 and rooftops, 56
 and west-facing
 balcony, 62
Sweet alyssum, 106
Sweet bay, 93
Sweet peas, 102
Sweet potato, 76
Syringa, 96

T
Tamarix aphyla, 60
Tarragon, 48
Taxus baccata, 22
Thuja, 93
Thyme, 48, 99
Thymus, 48, 99
Tomatoes, 48, 78
Topiary, 22
Tracery, 22
Trailing plants, 100, 107
Trees, 89-95
 abuse, withstanding,
 95
 for cold climates, 94
 color for more than
 one season, 94
 dwarf, 80, 81, 85
 fragrant small, 95
 for mild climates, 93,
 94
 and shade, 51
 shrubs trained into, 95

Trident maple, 90
Tristania laurina, 94
Trough gardens, 13,
 28, 29
Trumpet creeper, 102
Tsuga, 44, 93
Tulips, 107

U
U.C. mix, 17

V
Vancouveria chrysanta,
 50, 51
Vegetables, 43, 75-79
 in containers, 48
 and raised beds, 21
 in shade, 52
Viburnums, 96
Vines, 89, 101-103
Violas, 106
 odorata, 50, 51
 tricolor hortensis, 52
Virginia creeper, 22, 101

W
Walls and raised beds,
 21
Water
 for balcony gardens,
 62
 for community
 gardens, 87
 for house gardens, 68
 infiltration rate, 16
 plants needing little, 70
 for rooftop gardens, 57
Watermelon, 78
Weeping forsythia, 22
Weight
 and balcony gardens,
 62
West-facing balcony, 62
White poplar, 94
Wild strawberry, 98
Wilson holly, 94
Wind
 and balconies, 60
 and rooftops, 56
Windowbox, 55, 72, 73
Winter creeper, 99, 101
Wire baskets and boxes,
 15
Wisterias, 102
 sinensis, 102
Woodsorrel, 50, 51

X
Xylosma, 97

Y
Yaupon holly, 94
Yew pine, 93

Z
Zinnias, 105